Bacon Sandwiches *and* Salvation

Bacon Sandwiches *and* Salvation

An A–Z of the Christian Life

Adrian Plass

LONDON • COLORADO SPRINGS • HYDERABAD

14 13 12 11 10 09 08 13 12 11 10 9 8

Reprinted 2007 (5), 2008 (twice)

First published 2007 by Authentic Media
9 Holdom Avenue, Bletchley, Milton Keynes, Bucks, MK1 1QR, UK
1820 Jet Stream Drive, Colorado Springs, CO 80921, USA
OM Authentic Media, Medchal Road, Jeedimetla Village,
Secunderabad 500 055, A.P., India
www.authenticmedia.co.uk
Authentic Media is a division of IBS-STL U.K., a company limited by guarantee, with its registered office at Kingstown Broadway, Carlisle, Cumbria CA3 0HA. Registered in England & Wales No.1216232. Registered charity 270162

British Library Cataloguing in Publication Data

A catalogue record for this book is available from the British Library

ISBN 978-1-85078-723-5

Cover Designed by James Kessell for Scratch the Sky Ltd.
(www.scratchthesky.com)
Print Management by Adare Carwin
Printed and bound by J.H. Haynes & Co., Sparkford

INTRODUCTION

The Sacred Diary of Adrian Plass had its birth in a regular feature on the inside back cover of *Christian Family Magazine*. *Bacon Sandwiches and Salvation* grew out of a column that appeared for several weeks on the back page of *The Baptist Times*. Similarities do not end there. The kind of nervous commitment ('panic' might be a better word) that I tend to put into the production of material for a column, especially one purporting to be amusing, is in some ways more urgent and painstaking than the energy required to begin a book from nothing. In each case that original material from the columns, although a small proportion of the completed work, has provided me with a sort of creative and imaginative racing start, and made the quest to compile an entire book that much more vital and exciting.

A word of explanation about the title of this book. I found myself next to my friend Liz in church one day. Liz and I are not really very good for each other in this situation. At our worst, we are like two naughty children messing about and making silly jokes at the back of the class. We have never actually been formally split up yet, but it could happen. Halfway through the service our minister asked the congregation a question.

'For you,' he asked, 'what is the most important thing in the world?'

Liz and I answered more or less simultaneously. My reply was very proper and holy for a change.

'Salvation!' I cried piously.

'Bacon sandwiches!' suggested Liz, with all the passion and wisdom you would expect from a retired magistrate and area schools advisor for religious education.

Yes, I thought to myself. Of course. Bacon sandwiches and salvation. That just about sums it up. A God who can create the indescribable tastiness of a bacon sandwich must be planning something pretty incredible in the salvation line. A title was born. Thanks, Liz.

I have had such fun with *Bacon Sandwiches*. I hope that most of it will make you laugh, or at least smile, and I also hope that you will not hurt yourself too badly when you trip over the occasional serious or whimsical bits. God bless you.

ASSYRIANS

A

Adam: first example of someone who ruined his life by taking banned substances that had been growing in his garden. It was his bird's idea, and she got nicked as well.

Afterlife: (1) something dreaded by those who believe it will be like one of their Sunday morning services, only going on for ever and ever. When you've sung *Shine Jesus Shine* for the nine millionth time . . . (2) a place where God will chew a straw and fill us in on how things really are (3) a time when, according to Oscar Wilde, good Americans will go to Paris and bad Americans will go to America.

Agape love: (1) Christian fellowship, especially as distinct from erotic love (2) kissing with your mouth open.

Agnostic: (1) a person who believes that nothing is known, or can possibly be known, of the existence or nature of God, or of anything beyond normal phenomena (2) Gnostic with a.

A growing time: ghastly phrase used as a verbal sticking plaster to cover a period of one's life that was so horrible, hopeless and apparently lacking in the presence and power of God that none of the other statutory religious terms will cover it.

Alcohol: substance recommended in moderation by Saint Paul for medical reasons connected with the stomach, in which case there must be an epidemic of severe gastric problems in certain sections of our present day evangelical culture.

Alpha: outreach system that has brought thousands to faith, but has left in its wake a small, deeply confused group of people who have mistakenly asked Nicky Gumbel into their lives.

Altar-ego: alternative persona adopted by Anglican priests during services.

And lastly: phrase employed by preachers, meaning 'Don't even think about so much as shifting in your chair, we've got a long way to go yet.'

And thirdly: used by preachers in their endless quest to prove that every single aspect of life has been divinely divided into three parts, each beginning with the same letter, as in 'Peace, Power and Pork-scratchings.'

Anglican: (1) a charismatic (2) an anti-charismatic (3) one who is in favour of women in the priesthood (4) one who is not in favour of women in the priesthood (5) one who has close links with Rome (6) one who abhors Rome (7) one who sees no problem with the ordination of gay clergy (8) one who is absolutely opposed to the ordination of gay clergy (9) one who has just arrived in hospital (10) one who turns to her neighbour when *Worthy is the Lamb* is being sung, and says, 'I hope the joint's big enough . . .' (11) an institution that has proved it can be laughed at and respected and loved by its members. If the song *These Foolish Things* was addressed to the Church of England, it might read as follows:

The folks arriving with their Sunday faces
The silent struggle for the back row places
The cloud the caretaker brings
These foolish things remind me of you

The rousing hymn before the three-point sermon
The verger's gran who sounds like Ethel Merman
We share our pain as she sings
These strangled things remind me of you

The winds of change, so many priests are female
The current vogue to be baptised by e-mail
Oh, how the pendulum swings
These trendy things remind me of you

Your spires, your choirs, your liturgy
These things are dear to me
The coffee's frightful, but it's always free

The hour's talk on what Mosaic Law meant
A short rehearsal for eternal torment
It dries up all our springs
These dusty things remind me of you

The invitation to the peace extended
Deep relaxation when the damn thing's ended
Such wretched murmurings
These awkward things remind me of you

Before communion the hesitation
A moment later it's like Euston Station
Perplexed meanderings
These puzzling things remind me of you

Sometimes, they say, why C of E?
I love the history
I love the muddle and the mystery

The flippant lad who likes to play the joker
He claims the Bible holds a hand at poker
Of course he means Two Kings
These stupid things remind me of you

The grace of God like summer rain descending
The hush that fills thc church seems never ending
Till someone's mobile rings
These ghastly things remind me of you

The autumn evensongs we all remember
Through years that fly like leaves in late September
The kiss of angels' wings
These tender things remind me of you.

Anglican Reform: (1) Back to Basics movement within the Church of England (2) gin canal.

Anthem: (1) elaborate choral composition based on a passage of Scripture (2) word that means 'good-looking' when used by a cockney with a lisp.

Apathy: driving force behind our attitudes to the Third World.

Apostle spoon: small cutlery item, usually featuring a tiny image of Saint Paul, presumably because his teaching caused such a stir.

Apple crumble: dish invented to commemorate Eve's temptation and the subsequent fall.

Armageddon: term used in game played by God with an off-duty angel, as in:
'Knock, knock!'
'Who's there?'
'Armageddon.'
'Armageddon who?'
'Armageddon tired of evil, let's have the last battle.'

A B C D E F G H I J K L M N O P Q R S T U V W X Y Z

Art: something regarded with deep suspicion by many folk in the church. This sad prejudice was exemplified at the Spring Harvest art gallery a few years ago, when someone wrote in the comments book: 'Too many bottoms for my liking.' Particularly frustrating when one reflects that most great art produced over the years was influenced or inspired by Christian belief.

As the Lord leads: fairly common phrase among Christians, meaning 'I haven't decided yet.'

Ascension: occasion recorded in the first chapter of the book of Acts when Jesus departed from his followers by being taken up and disappearing into a cloud. A highly significant and reassuring event for Christians, as it demonstrates the preservation of the individual person in the spiritual realm. Those who doubt the sanity of Christian belief, however, might be tempted to adapt the latter part of the story to suit their views:

After he saith this, behold he was taken up before their very eyes, and an cloud hideth him from their sight.

They were looking intently up into the sky as he was going, when, behold, suddenly two men dressed in white standeth beside them. And the disciples explaineth excitedly that their master hath disappeared into the sky.

One of the two men replieth soothingly, 'Well, of course he hath, gentlemen, right up into the sky. We doubteth it not. Now, if thou wilt climbeth quietly up into the back of this nice white van that we have broughteth for thine transport, we shall take thee to an peaceful place where thou canst safely stare up into the sky to thine hearts' desire. Cometh along now. No trouble.'

'And,' enquireth one of the disciples, his eyes bright as he pauseth before stepping into the van, 'wilt there be an upper room in this place of which thou speakest, where we may gather and wait to be clothed with power from on high?'

'Upper room?' saith one of the white-coated men. 'Funny thou shouldst saith that. Why, verily we specialiseth in upper rooms, don't we, George? All you gentlemen canst sit up there in one of our upper rooms with the nice soft walls and the en-suite facilities and be clothed in power from on high or in Widow Twanky costumes or Lithuanian bus conductors' uniforms, or whatsoever thou wisheth. Now moveth it along, there's a good disciple, or we shall arriveth late for supper. Thine er master sitting up there in the cloud mighteth not be too happy about that.'

And he winketh heavily at George . . .

Ashurbanipal: a name slipped into the fourth chapter of Ezra by God for the purpose of preserving humility in those who think they are such good sight readers that they don't need to prepare the Sunday lesson.

Assyrians: an aggressive people who always seemed to be sweeping down from somewhere and never sweeping back up, although, when you think about it, they must have swept back up at some point in order to be in a position to sweep down again, mustn't they?

Astrology: the study of the movement and relative positions of celestial bodies interpreted as an influence on human affairs. In other words, the one that's not all right. And of course as Christians we just thank our lucky stars that there's no need for us to get involved with such things.

Astronomy: the one that is all right. Patrick Moore may be somewhat eccentric, but he is not the High Priest of the occult movement.

Atheist: (1) lapsed agnostic (2) someone who, according to Chesterton, settles for exploring mazes that have neither a centre nor an exit.

'Avoid London – Area closed – Turn on radio': extraordinary and not at all funny disaster-movie-style sign presented to my wife and I and thousands of other drivers negotiating the M25 on 7/7/05, the day when bombers brought terror to the city of London. We were on our way to Luton (the station from which the terrorists began their journey) to meet our daughter, who was travelling through the capital city by train at the exact time when the explosions occurred. She arrived safely and was unharmed. Many were not. Life was never to be the same for huge numbers of victims, relatives and friends.

BACKSLIDING

B

Babes and sucklings: Minor Prophets.

Babylon: (1) city situated on the river Euphrates to which the Israelites were exiled (2) what a lot of preachers do.

Backsliding: activity shared by wavering Christians and penguins. Both likely to get into deep water as a result, the difference being that the penguins look forward to doing it again a little less than the Christians.

Bacon sandwiches: a seriously neglected evangelistic tool. Imagine if bacon were to be fried at the front of outreach rallies as the evangelist is speaking. The smell would, of course, be heavenly. Members of the congregation would be informed that any person coming forward to make a commitment automatically receives a free bacon sandwich. There would be a stampede to the front. Bacon sandwiches and salvation. What an unbeatable and eminently Jesus-like combination! (See also *Salvation*).

Baguette: (1) long thin loaf of bread (2) word used by the French in biblical genealogies, as in:

Solomon baguette Rehoboam,
Rehoboam baguette Abijah,
Abijah baguette Asa . . . etc.

Balaam's ass: part of Balaam, in the sense that he became deeply attached to the creature.

Bangladesh: country where five million children struggle to stay alive every day. Hardly a religious subject. Move on quickly.

Baptist Church: denomination in which one senses that there is an awful lot going on under the surface.

Barking: apparent feature of a comparatively recent wave of blessing in the church that has given rise to such snatches of dialogue as:

A: (overcome by whatever it is) Woof! Woof!
B: Why are you doing that?
A: I'm barking.
B: Ah, yes, I suppose that would explain it . . .

Be bold: chorus sung by Christian cricket fans when the Australians are batting. Until recently not a very helpful activity for those who are looking to build up their faith. A different story since 2005!

Be of one mind: a good idea as long as it isn't taken to mean that the one mind has to be divided up in equal parts between all eighty-six members of the congregation.

Beatitude: (1) declaration of blessedness in Matthew's gospel. Certain omissions are much regretted by modern Christians, e.g. 'Blessed are the couch potatoes, for they shall be brought snacks.' (2) not to be confused with a similar phrase widely used in marriage: 'I am so sick and tired of your whole B. attitude.'

Behemoth: (1) hippopotamus or elephant mentioned in the book of Job (2) identification instruction given to a member of the Lepidoptera family by Adam when he was naming the animals.

Benediction: (1) blessing at the end of a service (2) strange vocal habits of old simpleminded *Crossroads* character who always wore a woolly hat.

Benjamite: (1) member of the tribe of Benjamin (2) early form of Israeli yeast extract that you either love or hate.

Bildad: (1) the Shuhite, one of Job's longwinded comforters (2) second part of his name suggests that he might have been an ancient maker of ankle-supporting boots (3) phrase completing a sentence frequently used by supposedly grown-up offspring to their fathers: 'Any chance of you paying this . . . '

Billy Graham: (1) anagram of 'Big rally ham' (2) sweet man of God, more effective at moving backsides in the right direction than the most popular and heavily patronised proctologist in the world.

Bind us together, Lord: grace sung before a meal of boiled eggs.

Bishop: (1) senior member of Christian clergy in charge of the diocese, a father to his people (2) one who is not capable of moving in any direction other than diagonally (3) character that is not supposed to behave like a pawn.

Bless you: clear off.

Blessed: (1) consecrated (2) less in bed (3) big, wide-faced, grumpy actor with annoyingly loud voice who climbs mountains.

Blessed are the wounds of a friend: phrase from the twenty-sixth chapter of Proverbs, occasionally quoted by those who have something extremely unfriendly to say.

Blind pew: (1) scary character in *Treasure Island*, by Robert Louis Stevenson, who delivers the 'black spot' (2) worst seat in Anglican church immediately behind a pillar.

Boaz: Ruthless Old Testament character, totally transformed by marriage.

Boredom: largely unacknowledged feature of church life. Worth bearing in mind that Jesus left people angry, puzzled, elated, entertained, fed, disgusted and overjoyed but, as far as we know, never bored.

Born again Christian: (1) person who has entered into a glorious new life with Christ (2) a tautology. The response to those who ask if one is a born again Christian might well be: 'What's the other sort, then?' (3) ill-mannered and misguided believers who try to stuff their boring beliefs down other people's throats. Not to labour the point, but perhaps those of us who have been remiss enough to unwittingly persuade non-Christians that the latter definition is the correct one should reflect on the fact that the famous nocturnal encounter in John's gospel between Jesus and Nicodemus did not proceed like this:

> Now there was a man of the Pharisees named Nicodemus, a member of the ruling council. He came to Jesus at night, and said, 'Rabbi, we know you are a teacher who has come from God. For no one could perform the miraculous signs you are doing if God were not with him.'
>
> In reply Jesus declared, 'I tell you the truth, no one can see the kingdom of God unless he becomes a bigoted narrow-minded git.'

Brainwashing: process by which contrary ideas can be planted in the mind: never used in the Christian church (special intensive courses are available for those who stubbornly refuse to believe this).

A B C D E F G H I J K L M N O P Q R S T U V W X Y Z

A B C D E F G H I J K L M N O P Q R S T U V W X Y Z

Bread of heaven: great and glorious provision which we Anglicans slice up neatly and use to make hymn sandwiches.

Breasts: described by Solomon (who was supposed to know about women) as being like two fawns browsing among lilies. One can only assume that some initial misconception was reinforced by the short-sighted king's devoted followers ensuring that each wife approached him backwards wearing a rucksack containing a bunch of flowers and a pair of hungry ferrets.

Bride of Christ: the church, a body that will be presented pure and unspotted to Christ. Well, when I say pure and unspotted, we don't always quite manage such perfection. Sometimes we are not even aware that we are falling short.

I remember sitting in a church that was not my own, listening to a heated exchange between people who, judging by the way they were speaking, must have felt a deep loathing for each other.

This was the Annual General Meeting of an evangelical church situated several miles from my hometown, and I had been invited to attend for a very specific purpose. The elders of this church were keen to put on an outreach event that would attract and draw in local people who would not otherwise darken (or lighten) the doors of the establishment. Apparently the whole congregation felt a strong desire to share the gospel with their neighbours. This being the case, they were wondering if Bridget and I might write and direct a Christian revue that would be genuinely entertaining, but would also provide the chance to make a clear, honest and unthreatening statement about Jesus. It was an interesting and intriguing proposition, and I had been more than happy to give some thought to the idea. I had been invited to the AGM so that, at some point in the second half of the proceedings, I could outline my ideas.

The meeting had been in progress now for about twenty-five minutes, and I had had to use an effort of the will to prevent my jaw from dropping in amazement. The chairman of the meeting was a good friend of mine, and he was doing a valiant job, but he was beginning to make Basil Fawlty look like a sedated nun, and I did not blame him in the slightest. I had rarely heard church people, or any people for that matter, being so unpleasant, obstructive, argumentative, loud and uncooperative. It was not the whole group of fifty or so church members who were behaving like this, but a sufficiently large minority to make this divine event feel acrimonious and uncomfortable, especially to a visitor.

The situation was made doubly irksome by the fact that one of the two main male troublemakers was a tall man who spoke in piercingly high falsetto tones, while the other was small and round and had a mechanical buzz of a voice, not dissimilar to the vibrating drone of a high-speed dentist's drill. These two individuals had a wide range of objecting skills. They objected to what was being said. They objected to the order in which these objectionable things were being said, and they objected to what was said in substitution for the things that were said, but were then objected to by them.

Additionally, they objected to the things that were not being said, and when, at their bidding, those things were said, they objected in the strongest possible terms to the manner in which they were said. If they had been told that every single one of their objections would be met in full, these people would have objected, because then there would have been nothing left to object about, and that would have left no reason for them to be alive, and how many of those present, I asked myself, could possibly have objected to that?

Perhaps my memory is failing me and I am exaggerating. Possibly, but only just. The conflict and bad feeling flying around in that room, not just from Squeaky and Buzzy but also from several others, had to be seen and heard to be believed. It was a relief to stop for refreshments.

At last teas and coffees had been consumed and it was my turn to stand up and address the AGM on the subject of the proposed revue. I looked around for a moment at the rows of faces in front of me. My ears were still ringing with the echoes of verbal artillery. Where should I start?

'Well,' I said at last, 'thank you for inviting me to your AGM, and I have to say straightaway that I really don't think you need an outreach revue at all.'

Brows met. Faces contracted with puzzlement. People looked at each other and shook heads. That was why I was there, wasn't it?

'No,' I continued, 'you don't have to bother with anything like that. Just invite all the local people to one of your AGMs and that should do the trick. They'll come here, listen to you sniping and objecting and taking offence, and they'll say, "Yes! Yes! This is what we want. Just to be part of a group of people like this who truly love each other. If this is what following Jesus means, then we want to be a part of it. Yes! Fantastic! When do we start? Where do we sign?"'

There was a moment of silence. Perhaps I had gone too far. Perhaps I should be minding my own business. But I was trying to be a follower of Jesus, and Jesus makes everything his business.

Somebody laughed. Another person laughed. Lots of people were laughing. I was not able to do a strictly accurate count, but I estimated that the laughers exceeded fifty percent of those present, and therefore the non-laughers were out-voted, and the unproposed but extremely important motion was invisibly carried:

'This AGM believes that we have been behaving in a very silly fashion and we ought not to let it happen again.'

All this provided an excellent platform for talking about the fact that, if we really wanted to reach out, we had to have some clear idea of what we were reaching out with. What do we Christians have that is worth offering to other people?

A B C D E F G H I J K L M N O P Q R S T U V W X Y Z

Bring and share lunches: largely responsible for the great quiche flood of 1964, in which many evangelical Christians came close to suffocating under the sheer weight of the huge number of tarts thronging church halls throughout the country.

Bull of Bashan: usual old nonsense that we've come to expect from Bashan.

Burn: less desirable option than to marry, according to Saint Paul, who somehow managed to live with the former and, as far as we know, never experienced the latter. Likely to be a lengthy and somewhat restless queue in heaven waiting to discuss this matter with the great apostle.

CHRISTENING SERVICE

Calvary: anagram of 'cavalry', a widely-used term for a person or group of people who effect a last-minute rescue from disaster. Has exactly the same meaning.

Calvinists: Christians whose theology suggests that they might not bother to book their hotel rooms in advance when planning a holiday because they are absolutely convinced that someone else will have done it for them, and if they haven't there's no use trying.

Camel: commonly described as a horse designed by a committee, as opposed to a Parochial Church Council, which is more like a committee designed by a camel.

Can I just say, in love: brace yourself.

Can of worms: (1) a mass of problems or difficulties that may be overwhelming if they are once investigated (2) presumably a frequent and essential requirement in the Diet of Worms.

Carvery church: place where you go up to the front, collect as much of what is on offer as you can, take it back to your seat, gobble it up, then go home and forget about it until next Sunday.

Censorship: sort of mine-sweeping vessel that lacks effectiveness when the captain refuses to employ depth-sounding equipment, but relies on the naked eye of someone who is scanning the surface from a very great height.

Change: rare phenomenon as far as the church is concerned, except when it comes to the collection. Tends to be fairly limited even then.

Charismatic: (1) healthily open to the work, the works and the gifts of the Holy Spirit (2) mad (3) likely to attend churches where freedom of expression is strictly enforced.

Cheese and pickle: according to most of the spiritual biographies I have read, great heroes of the Christian faith are continually experiencing and witnessing mighty miracles, either in the physical world around them or in their own personalities. In fact, in the latter area there appears to be such a weeping and a breaking down and a blackness and a blinding light and a despairing and a rejoicing and a succession of starkly dramatic confrontations with the power and presence of the living God that it is difficult to see how the central characters ever have time to eat or sleep or go to the toilet or do their laundry. Bearing in mind the cosmic scale and nature of these events I hardly like to record the fact that my last meaningful encounter with the Creator of the universe directly concerned half a pound of mature Cheddar cheese and a jar of Branston pickle.

Let me explain.

I was appearing on the late night fringe at the big Christian festival called Spring Harvest, and had therefore been allocated a chalet to stay in. Arriving at my chalet, and having used up every single point of my meagre I.Q. on working out how to unlock the door, I discovered it to be reasonably comfortable and well-equipped. However, there were another two twin bedrooms besides my own, as well as a communal sitting room, kitchen and bathroom. During the next few hours other people would undoubtedly appear, after which there could be as many as five of us sharing all these facilities.

Now, I have to be honest. I am not the world's best at sharing living space with others. Given the choice nowadays I opt for the sweet anonymity of hotel dwelling rather than being a domestically dysfunctional visitor in the houses of people I do not know. My wife Bridget is much better at it than I am. She is genuinely warm and kind. I have to role-play a bit sometimes. Nevertheless, on this occasion I actually had worked on preparing myself to be ready and willing to face the people who were to be my chalet-mates.

As I unpacked my case, hung up clothes, distributed bits and pieces with neurotic exactitude around the room and put my two books (one deep and useful volume that I ought to be reading and one superficial load of rubbish that I was actually engrossed in) on the bedside table, I asked myself what I should do next.

'Why not eat?'

It was my stomach speaking. I had eaten almost nothing since setting out that morning, and I was more than ready for a snack.

Cue the aforesaid cheese and pickle.

I always take a stash of food with me when I am away from home. If I am staying with people there is always the possibility that they will eat like anorexic sparrows and assume that I am likely to do the same. A couple of sandwiches and a piece of cake can make all the difference, especially when they are consumed (with low volume chewing over an open broadsheet newspaper) as a sort of midnight feast in the privacy and intimidating perfection of the guest bedroom. At places like Spring Harvest they give you food vouchers that can be exchanged for goods at the on-site store, which is fine if you remember to get everything you want while you are there. Sometimes the chalets, delightful as they may be, are quite a long way from the centre. Forgetting some crucial item and having to brave cloudbursts or blizzards to do an Amundsen-style trek up to the shop and back again can be a dreary business.

Hence my stash.

On this occasion I had tea-bags, coffee, sugar, milk, a box of individual French Fancies, a steak and kidney pie, a packet of Hobnob biscuits, a loaf of bread, one of those tubs of marge with a ridiculously long name and (roll of drums!) a wedge of cheese and a jar of pickle.

I got it all out and arranged it on a shelf in my room, then stood back and, Gollum-like, surveyed my precious, my sweetly private store of sustenance. This food was *mine*. All *mine*. *My* tea and coffee and stuff, *my* cakes and biscuits and, crucially because I enjoyed it so much, *my* cheese and pickle. Not a single item from my portable larder was going to find its way into the communal kitchen, because if it did – well, it was obvious, wasn't it? People would use it. We all know what *people* are like, for goodness sake! They would empty my carton of milk, ravage my biscuits and cakes, share my pie out in crudely hacked slices and, horror of horrors, they would make great thick cheese sandwiches, smothered with far more pickle than they actually needed because they hadn't paid for it. Oh, no! This stuff was going to stay right where it was and if they didn't bring their own, it was hard luck.

Now, in case you think this is an exaggeration, I am afraid I have to disappoint you. It's odd in

A B C D E F G H I J K L M N O P Q R S T U V W X Y Z

a way. Those who know me best would, I believe, describe me as quite a generous person, but every now and then I stumble into little pockets of narrow-eyed miserliness in my own personality. I was at a Christian conference, all geared up to speak with humour and passion about the business of following Jesus, and here was this shrivelled little moral gnome of a person inside me, rubbing his hands with selfish glee as he gloated over possessions that he had no intention of sharing with anyone else.

This obvious contradiction hit me quite suddenly, a bit like a bucket of water landing unexpectedly on my head.

'What on *earth* are you doing?' I asked myself out loud. 'You spend your life bleating about the implications of being a Christian, and here you are planning to keep your miserable little stash of food hidden away in the corner of your miserable little room so that no one else can get their hands on it. You pillock!'

I couldn't help chuckling to myself as I transferred my comestibles to the communal kitchen, partly because the way God operates often makes me laugh, and partly because if this story had happened two thousand years ago and subsequently been included in Holy Writ, I suppose it would have been solemnly entitled The Parable of the Cheese and Pickle.

Chicken in a basket: culinary dish invented to mark the occasion when Paul was lowered down over a wall to escape the Jews.

Choruses: Christian songs that quite often tempt one to change a crucial line, as in:

> The name of the Lord is
> A strong tower
> The righteous run into it
> And bang their heads.

Or perhaps to change it quite innocently, like the little girl who after years of cutting and making and sticking in the children's groups, sang out at the top of her voice:

'Come on, let's sellotape, sellotape, sellotape and string!'

Some choruses seem to be based on obscure sections of Old Testament Scripture, and are sung with a sort of maniacal intensity by people who surely cannot be altogether clear about what the words mean:

> We raise our elbows to the ephod in the sanctuary,
> We cleanse our gourds from water pots that once were sealed,
> We gather at the sacred stones of Zebulon
> Where the sons of Eli's nephews will be healed.
>
> And they who once were not will not be not now,
> And they who were will now no longer be,
> And they who thought they were will now know that they are not,
> And the whole thing will remain a mystery.
>
> And I must go and feed my kangaroo now,
> He's juggling LEGO on the kitchen range
> He's changed his name from Albert to Virginia,
> I think I need a week at Ellel Grange . . .

A B C D E F G H I J K L M N O P Q R S T U V W X Y Z

A B C D E F G H I J K L M N O P Q R S T U V W X Y Z

Christ: (1) the Name above all Names, who gave himself for us and for our salvation (2) a common swear word.

Christening service: naming and dedication ceremony in some of the traditional denominations. Attending non-Christian relatives and friends can easily be identified by the fact that they are so much more smartly dressed than the regular congregation.

Christian bookshops: places offering a wide range of narrow literature, and usually called something with 'vine' in it. Hence: The Vine. The Fruit of the Vine. Vine leaves. Vine branch. Vine Harvest. Grapevine. Off the Vine. On the Vine. Up the Vine. Down the Vine. Round the Vine. Tucked round the back of the Vine. Plucked from the Vine. Dropped from the Vine. Root of the Vine. Wine from the Vine. Unfermented Grape juice from the Vine . . .

Christian dance: (1) at its best, the inspiring and uplifting use of a powerful art form (2) something that fails miserably when its exponents adhere too rigidly to guidelines taken from chapter fifteen, section nine of *The Official Handbook of Christian Postures and Practices,* which states the following:

> It should be borne in mind by all choreographers and participants that only four postures or movements are allowed in Christian dance.
>
> The first of these is known as the *Please heal me, one of my arms is much longer than the other* pose. This involves one cupped hand being extended outward and upwards as far as it will go in an

imploring gesture, while the other, similarly cupped, is drawn back against the chest.

Next comes the *Unwatered plant* posture, in which the dancers droop down onto the floor with their heads hung on their chests and both hands trailing limply on the floor like dehydrated vegetation.

Thirdly there is the *Whatever that cream was I just put on my face, it doesn't half sting* position, requiring the palms of both hands to be placed flat against the face so that all features are obscured.

Finally, dancers may use the *One of my hands is trying to run away from me and I am reluctantly forced to chase trippingly after it in little circles* movement.

Any combination or permutation of these components is permissible, but there must never at any time be the slightest suggestion that the dancers are anything but androgynous beings, skilled in the art of 'Sexless wafting' as an expert has termed it.

Christian magazines: with one or two notable exceptions, something of a dying breed nowadays. Characterised in the old days by articles with such titles as 'Mowing The Lawn The Christian Way.' Pieces like this would usually include a box set into the centre of one page of the article containing six handy hints for 'Christian mowers.' These might consist of:

(1) Do bear in mind that mowers can be noisy things. Does your neighbour have a small child who may be sleeping? Why not call over the fence or go round and ring the front door bell to ask? Bang on the

A B C D E F G H I J K L M N O P Q R S T U V W X Y Z

windows if necessary. Don't give up. Be persistent. Consideration for others is a part of outreach.

(2) Mowing the lawn can offer a great opportunity for witnessing. If your neighbour is also cutting his grass or relaxing in his garden after a hard day at work, why not lean over the fence and, in a natural sort of way, start up a conversation about the Lord?

(3) If such a conversation does get going, perhaps as a result of your neighbour spotting a selection of fish stickers strategically attached to the front and sides of your mower, casually point out to him that, just as your grass will be cut and eventually dumped on the compost heap at the end of the garden, so his sins can be removed and disposed of in exactly the same way.

(4) Remember that we are called upon to be good stewards in all areas of our lives. If yours is a cylinder mower, why not turn it off each time you pull it towards you, and turn it on again for each forward stroke? This will honour God, and certainly have a profound effect on your neighbour, who will experience a growing awareness that you are not as other men.

(5) Why not start up a Christian lawn mowing club with other chaps from your church? Ask your unsaved neighbour if he would like to come along to one of the meetings. Tell him it is just a group of fellows sitting around in their shirtsleeves, admiring and comparing each others' mowers, drinking a glass (or two!) of Shloer together, and discussing such subjects as the best fuel to use in their machines. It will be easy to progress from there to asking him what fuels his life and gently letting him know what fuels yours. After the first of these meetings look him straight in the eye and tell him that he is only a step away from becoming just like you and your friends.

(6) Make a special study of the fortieth chapter of Isaiah in which we are taught that 'all men are like grass'. Reflect on the fact that the Bible is to be taken literally. Be bold and obedient. Paint yourself bright green from head to toe, bury your feet in the lawn and call your neighbour over to observe that the word of Scripture is indeed fulfilled. By now he should be on the edge of seriously contemplating a move.

One or two of the magazines seem to have changed their names with feverish regularity in the hope of attracting a new readership. Perhaps they are too positive. Is it possible that negative titles would be more successful? We might, for instance, have *Decay* instead of *Renewal, Omega* instead of *Alpha*. And I for one would certainly rush out to buy any Christian magazine that called itself *Sour Grapes*. What about *Christianity Tomorrow*? And how does *Woman Dead* sound?

Yes, all right, I've stopped . . .

Christian speaker: (1) someone who has only ever had problems in the past (2) one who always does their best to ensure that they speak from a lack of personal experience.

Christmas: a season when it is possible for Christians and everybody else to hear one person's voice more clearly and more frequently than at any other time in the year, and, of course, it's a nice little earner for him – Noddy Holder, that is.

A B C D E F G H I J K L M N O P Q R S T U V W X Y Z

Christmas Carol Service: (1) a warm, wonderful, innovative way to celebrate the birth of Christ (2) yet another tediously predictable way of postponing the next issue of mince pies during the Christmas season.

Circumcision: painful cut-off point between Jews and Gentiles.

Clay pots: the apostle Paul's description of what we are in relation to the Divine Potter. Might go some way towards explaining the glazed expression that so many of us wear.

Cleave: what the marriage service says husbands and wives are supposed to do to each other, preferably not with a cleaver.

Clerical collar: arrest of a clergyman.

Coffee: the weak but welcome light at the end of the tunnel in just about every church-related situation that human beings have ever been in.

Communion – Anglican and Roman Catholic: the time when people leave their sins and spectacles on their seats as they line up for a tiny taste of the glory of God.

Communion – most others: the time when people sit on their sins and spectacles and have a tiny taste of the glory of God delivered to them.

Condemnation: infinitely preferable to long-winded and inappropriate ministry.

Condomnation: what Roman Catholics are likely to fall under if they use birth control.

Conference: common Christian event, presumably so-called because if not properly organised, it can so easily go pear-shaped.

Confessing, one to another: very laudable, useful and scripturally recommended activity. You just have to be very sure indeed that 'another' can keep their mouth shut about what 'one' has been brave or foolish enough to tell them.

Conversion: glorious process of positive change initiated and brought to fruition by (1) the Holy Spirit (2) Johnny Wilkinson (3) annoyingly handy people in lofts.

Covenant: (1) agreement between God and the Israelites (2) insect involved in black magic.

Crèche helmet: type of protective headwear that should be compulsorily worn during perilous work with very small children in church.

Criticism: something everyone says they welcome and need, but actually hated by ninety-nine per cent of us. Constructive criticism is particularly unpopular, because, having received it, we are likely to feel tediously obligated to do something about it.

Cross: (1) absurdly sentimentalised instrument of torture and death. Chances of Jesus having a secret hankering to get back to 'the old rugged cross' are really rather small. The point is emphasised if we imagine eating hot-garotte-buns at Easter time (2) the burden of sacrifice that each of us needs to take up daily if we are serious about following Jesus. May possibly involve a little more than being patient while last minute hitches in our mortgage arrangements are sorted out.

Crusades: (1) anagram of 'sad curse' (2) what the president of the United States of America so intelligently and usefully announced that he was conducting against terrorism and the Taliban a few years ago.

Curate: clergy assistant who learns through his vicar's mistakes.

DAVID JENKINS

D

Daddy: what the Bible tells us we're allowed to call God, which is a shame when you consider many of his adherents think of him as either a jailer, a headmaster, a bank manager, a sadist, a senile old man or a pathetically permissive sort of hippie.

Daily Bible notes: pieces of prose written in a deadline-driven, panic-stricken fever of hopeless despair at the very last possible moment, so that readers of the notes will be able to take a step back from their busy schedules and relax with God each day.

Damnation: (1) condemnation to eternal punishment (2) Holland.

Daniel: early vegan, so passionate and determined in his beliefs that he even seems to have managed to convert fierce wild carnivores to vegetarianism.

Darwin: (1) scientist and originator of the theory of the evolution of species by the action of natural selection. Likely, if he were to return, to be lynched (in love) by some shiny-eyed ones who are constantly seeking opportunities to express the Grace of God (2) term of endearment used by person lacking a roof to their mouth. As in, 'I love you, darwin.'

David: great Old Testament king of Israel who was hoping that he might be able to have his cake and sleep with it. Shepherd boy, musician, poet, giant-killer, warrior, wild naked dancer, murderer, adulterer and failed father, the Bible assures us that he was a man after God's own heart.

David Jenkins: ex-Bishop of Durham who captained a diocesan football team which was constantly disqualified because Jenkins would shrilly insist that the referee was only present in a symbolic sense.

Dear departed: expensive cause of funeral.

Dearly beloved: phrase used at the beginning of a sermon. In the case of ministers who are embattled and embittered, it may be interpreted as meaning 'Ladies and gentlemen of the jury.'

Deeply moved: what Christian speakers tell themselves their audiences and congregations must be when the only other alternative is that they are either bored or in a state of paralysed, blank incomprehension.

Defying gravity: (1) refusing to stay on the ground when there's even a slight possibility of being allowed to fly (2) what at least a few of us so-called followers of Jesus need to be doing. Christianity is far too serious not to be laughed at from time to time.

Den: (1) dirty, dank cave where Daniel finally faced his pride (2) dirty, dank character who never faced anything in early and late episodes of *Eastenders*.

Denominations: anagram of 'not made in Sion.' Further reading on this subject might include *No sects please, we're British, Sects and the single woman* and *The joy of sects*.

Devastation: place where you catch the train at Deva.

Directors for the singers: extract from Nehemiah 12:46 suggesting that the habit of supplying beer to musicians was as common then as it is now.

Disestablishmentarianism: (1) way of thinking that is strongly resisted and rejected by those who are lifelong, passionate supporters of antidisestablishmentarianism (2) a word most of us tried to learn and show off with when we were kids because it was so long.

'Divine' crescendo: a phenomenon that occurs quite frequently among Christians in the course of such activities as prayer, worship and the exercise of spiritual gifts. There appears to be a widespread misconception that God is more likely

A B C D E F G H I J K L M N O P Q R S T U V W X Y Z

to hear and respond to such communications when the voices of his followers rise gradually in volume and intensity until the speakers sound as if they are in danger of exploding. Sometimes it can be a corporate effort. I witnessed a striking example of this on a hot evening in the West Country several years ago.

The event was, as far as I can remember, a Pentecostal rally of some kind, a combined act of worship at the end of a day of seminars and teaching. After a number of hymns and choruses a man stood up to deliver a prophecy to the assembled company. Nothing wrong with that, of course. Prophecy is definitely one of the gifts of the Spirit, and the more we needy folk can hear from God, the better. Problems do arise, however, when group momentum, wishful thinking and mild hysteria take over from common sense. The sort of heavenly pictures where green beetles quiver gently on church steps can puzzle and depress the most open-minded of congregations.

So, what about the message (or messages) delivered on this occasion? Was God getting in touch with someone in the congregation, or was it another instance of over-enthusiastic humanity getting a bit carried away? I shall leave you to decide that for yourself.

The first man's prophecy was reasonably sane and restrained in tone.

'I see a fireplace,' he said, 'and the flames are growing smaller, so that there is no heat as there was before. Feed the fire before it dies completely. So saith the Lord.'

Apart from a peculiar reversion to sixteenth or seventeenth century language in the final part of the prophecy this seemed quite reasonable and helpful, whether it came directly from God or not. There must have been at least one person in that large crowd who needed fuel added to the fire of their spiritual life. Probably more than one. Lots, I expect. But as the first man resumed his seat a second one rose. This man's voice climbed onto a ledge just above the one occupied by the first.

'The fire is very low now! The fuel is consumed and has not been replaced. Bring fuel to the fire while yet it may be brought to life. The time is short and I will not always strive with you, says the Lord. Hear my words and obey my will, that the fire may be saved.'

Well, if it had ended there it might have been all right. I didn't like the 'will not always strive' bit. People seem to use this phrase far too easily, and with a strange sort of satisfaction. The Bible says that neither death nor life, nor angels nor demons, nor the present nor the future, nor any powers, nor height nor depth, nor anything else in all creation, will be able to separate us from the love of God that is in Christ Jesus our Lord. How could a bit of fuel neglect destroy our relationship when all those other things couldn't? However, there we are. The point about letting God reignite our lives had been well made. Twice. On to the next hymn, eh?

But no. Before anything else could happen a third, heavily bearded prophet rose like a behemoth from his place in the centre of the seated saints.

This fellow took the vocal effects to another level altogether. Like one of those old-fashioned, pre-microphone, theatrical types, he allowed his baritone voice to roar and wobble and quiver with doom-laden emotion. Compared to this bloke, Donald Wolfit was a deaf mute with a confidence problem.

'I see the place where the burning coals once were!' he raved, 'and they no longer burn! Go ye to the place wherein fuel may be got and bring it to the hearth so that it may be unto the lost a source of light and power! Oh, do not delay lest ye be found wanting in the final hour!'

It was after this that things got very silly indeed. If you can have such a thing as a religious bandwagon, then quite a lot of people climbed on it that evening. Hearing so many people deliver virtually the same message, it struck me that if this went on unchecked, the poor embattled sap whose fire was going out would end up being the only one left in the hall who hadn't prophesied about himself.

The end came when a tall, thin man with an aggressively bad haircut and a jacket whose sleeves ended halfway down his unnaturally hairy forearms unfolded himself from his chair like one of those old-fashioned three-foot wooden rulers and proceeded to add his three penn'orth to what had gone before. By now the tone and volume of successive prophesies had risen to such a hysterical pitch that the sound produced by this earnest brother was a sort of maniacal warble. Imagine *Carry On* star Kenneth Williams attempting to attract the attention of someone half a mile away after filling his lungs with helium, and you would be getting somewhere close.

'I see the ashes, and they're co-o-o-ld! They're so co-o-o-old! Oh, the ashes, the ashes in the cold grate! See the ashes! They're co-o-o-old! It's all so co-o-o-old! Everything is so –'

At this point, not before time in my view, the service leader decided that enough was enough.

'Yes, all right,' he interrupted at the microphone, a faint tinge of irritation adding an edge to his resonantly authoritative tone, 'I think we've probably got the message . . . '

Yes, I think we probably had. Someone's fire was going out, and if they hadn't got the message by now they probably never would.

Assuming that the original communication really was from God, I sometimes ask myself how the person concerned dealt with the crazy crescendo that followed. Lacking the slightest clue to that person's identity, I suppose I must accept that I will never know.

By the way, in case it occurs to you to ask, it was definitely not me . . .

Doctrine: (1) what they do up the Health Centre (2) the things that I believe, not to be confused with heresy, which is the things other people believe.

Doggerel: poetic form frequently favoured by Christians for reasons not easy to comprehend. Results vary, but in their worst form can be memorably dreadful, as in the following:

Becoming a Christian made me really radiant
As though I'd just come hurrying up a very steep gradient
Though my bright face wasn't caused by steep paths paved or unpaved
But by the fact that I had just been saved
What the future might hold for me has not yet been revealed
So I, and this applies to all of us, must keep my spiritual eyes peeled
All will be well I have no doubt in God's own good time
For he has forgiven my every sin, or, to use a different term, crime.

Dogma: (1) principle, tenet or system laid down by the church (2) anagram of 'go mad' (3) producer of canine litter.

Door: means of metaphorical entrance and exit that God appears to spend much of his time frenziedly opening and shutting in the lives of believers who are paralysed without inch-by-inch guidance.

Doubt: (1) more or less frequent visitor who should be allowed in when he knocks at the door and sat firmly down in a corner. As long as he is neither fed nor entertained he will usually get bored after a while and go away (2) often a very useful stepping stone from one's old distorted image of God to something a little more like the real thing. Not easy to accept, but a crucial aspect of change for the better in the lives of most Christians at one time or another (3) a well known evangelical theologian recently stated that anyone who believes Jesus never doubted his own divinity has failed to understand the New Testament.

A B C D E F G H I J K L M N O P Q R S T U V W X Y Z

EXCHANGING THE PEACE

Easter eggs: edible reminders of the resurrection, made of chocolate, filled with sweets and wrapped in shiny coloured paper, just as Our Lord was.

Eat, drink and be merry, for tomorrow we die: philosophy of life that departs just a tad from the teaching of Christ, but very accurately describes the combination of materialism and doubt that one supposes must underlie the so-called Prosperity Movement.

Ecstasy: experienced by thousands every Saturday night and by relatively fewer every Sunday morning, depending on where you go and who or what you worship.

A B C D E F G H I J K L M N O P Q R S T U V W X Y Z

Egg: (1) traditional symbol of eternity that takes four minutes to boil and three minutes to eat (2) food item tested for freshness exactly as witches were tested for guilt in medieval times. If they sink, they're good. If they float, they're bad.

Eggshell: where all those floating bad eggs go.

Emetics: possible name for one of the many courageous Christian bands who bravely refuse to allow lack of talent and skill to block the path of their ministry. A musical group called *The Emetics* could perform a very useful service for those who have always felt they have something inside them that really needs to come out.

End times: (1) an obsession on the part of those wild-eyed characters who, despite Jesus' clear statement that not even he knows when final judgement will come, continue to insist that the world will definitely end next Monday at exactly three twenty-seven in the afternoon, but refuse to give you any of their things, even though they obviously won't be needing them any more after the weekend (2) hairdressing and chiropody appointments.

Envy: sin mentioned in a passage in Romans that also includes homosexuality, greed and murder. Openly admitting to being envious was more or less taboo for Christians and non-Christians alike until the mid-sixties, when a few people came out of the closet and confessed to their inclinations. Nowadays, of course, debate rages in the Anglican Church and elsewhere about the suitability of ordaining those who publicly espouse the envious lifestyle.

A B C D E F G H I J K L M N O P Q R S T U V W X Y Z

Ephesians: book of the New Testament that has acquired a certain fame for thwarting those who claim to have heard from the Lord during Bible-study groups. As in:

A: (*in a low impressive voice*) I think the Lord is saying that we should look at Ephesians, chapter seven.
B: (*after a little immediate research, and with deep and sinful relish*) Oh, well, here's a bit of a problem, there are only six chapters in Ephesians.
A: (*redly, but with stubborn determination*) Ah, well, obviously he must have meant the first chapter of Philippians.

Epilogue: listening to this five minute talk at the end of the evening was the price paid in the sixties and seventies by non-Christian teenagers like me for chatting up girls and using other attractive facilities offered by church youth clubs.

Error: I was in Brighton, helping to prepare a church auditorium for an evening that Bridget and I were helping with. It was being held on behalf of a local residential establishment that catered for severely handicapped young people. The buzz of co-operation and mutual involvement was rather pleasant. I love it when the body of Christ is just pottering about humming to itself in such a way. I was in the middle of shifting a table from one side of the stage to another, when one of the ladies came up to me and said she had something to tell me.

'You'll find this funny,' she said.

I enjoy funny things and the table was heavy. I smiled and clunked the table down onto the wooden floor, glad of an excuse to stop doing anything for a minute or two. I leaned on it while I listened.

'The other day,' explained the lady, 'I was in my church and they were playing really loud instruments, things like guitars and drums and saxophones. Afterwards this woman came up to me at the back looking a bit – well, you know, a bit sour, arms folded and with her lips all pursed, and asked what I thought of the music. She obviously wasn't really interested in what I thought, though, because she never gave me a chance to answer. "Well, I'll tell you what I think," she said, "I think that if Jesus had been here he would have turned in his grave".'

My informant was absolutely right. I did find her story extremely funny. It would be hard to imagine a more comprehensively error-filled statement than the one made by that disapproving lady. She might just have been missing the point. For a start, Jesus was there. Secondly, he was and is not in his grave. Thirdly, for all we know he might have really enjoyed the music. I wondered if, in between worrying about us, God finds us as funny as we find each other. I hope so.

Eutychus: young man sitting on a window ledge who dropped off, literally, during one of Paul's long, long talks, and fell to his death. He was then kindly brought back to life by Paul so that he would not miss the end of the talk. The writer of Acts does not record how Eutychus reacted to this privilege, nor whether he was given any choice in the matter.

Evangelist: (1) those who preach the Gospel with a view to enabling their listeners to place their faith in Christ. The best are wonderful. I thank God for Denis Shepherd who triggered my own conversion forty years ago (2) an ego-bound Christian speaker who leans one arm challengingly on lecterns, beats the air with his forefinger and finds it impossible to believe that anyone can understand or absorb anything unless it's said thirty-nine times (2) anagram of 'Elvis agent' and 'gentle visa' and 'vital genes' and 'silage vent.'

Eve: (1) thrown out of the garden with Adam after the most ill-judged act of scrumping in history. Quoted, according to obscure sources, as saying, 'Yes, of course we've thought about creeping back into the blinking place, but just look at that flaming sword!' (2) presumably doomed to spend eternity at the gates of heaven, personally and profusely apologising to everyone who enters for every rotten thing that's ever happened to them.

Everlasting arms: (1) biblical image of the strength and comforting security of God's love (2) first pub on the left as you enter the Eternal City.

Every Day with Jesus: excellent daily Bible notes written by Selwyn Hughes. Future publications for the lazier believers among us might usefully include *Every other day with Jesus* or *Once a week if I remember with*

Jesus or *Random days in no particular pattern with Jesus* or even *It's ages since I spent any time at all with Jesus.*

Evil spell: any length of time spent in a French public toilet, a Scottish music festival, a Welsh pub or a shopping precinct in a small English town.

Evolution: survival of the fittest. A crucial issue for debate, no doubt, but a little alarming for those of us who are only just embarking on revival of the fattest (See also *Fat of the land*).

Exchanging the Peace: section of the Anglican communion service which induces sweaty palms and inward panic in those of us who are not sure whether to greet (a) the entire congregation (b) just the people we know (c) the ones sitting in the rows in front and behind or (d) nobody at all, which can be achieved by sitting quietly with your eyes closed, looking as if you are praying for everybody in the church.

Further tension is generated by the question of whether those we greet should be (a) hugged (b) kissed (c) shaken hands with (d) clapped on the shoulder in a matey sort of way or (e) waved to across the heads of others. How good it is to have this relaxing little informal episode in the midst of a traditional service.

Extracts: (1) small portions of, for instance, Scripture (2) emergency toilet paper.

Ezekiel: Old Testament prophet who, according to the *Swing Low* spiritual song, was removed by God from the earth in a heavenly vehicle approximating to a Tate & Lyle lorry.

FLOWER ROTA

F

Fads and fashions: quite an array of these in the church over recent years, including falling over, mooing, grunting, barking, laughing, shaking and having fillings replaced with gold, to name but a few. Unreliable rumours suggest the emergence of even more extraordinary manifestations of the Spirit such as care for the elderly, long-term kindness, justice, hospitality and help for the starving. Such rumours are wildly improbable and can safely be ignored.

Fall: (1) came early in Eden (2) apple picking season.

Family news letter: annual communication sent out by people whose children do well in exams.

A B C D E F G H I J K L M N O P Q R S T U V W X Y Z

Family worship: a television in every room.

Fanatics: (1) persons filled with excessive and often misguided enthusiasm over something (2) term often applied to Christians who are arrogant and insensitive enough to let others see that, to some small degree, their faith actually affects the way in which they live.

Fat of the land: (1) wealth and prosperity, as offered to Joseph and his family by Pharaoh in the forty-fifth chapter of Genesis (2) source of profit for thousands of gymnasiums and fitness clubs all over the country.

Feelings: negative, unreliable, misleading and irrelevant in the context of Christian experience, according to many teachers and preachers. And how right they are! One can only express wildly passionate, tearful agreement with this view.

Fellowship: (1) community of Christian interest (2) all-male cruise.

Fête: almost exclusively English institution. An outdoor money-raising event espoused by many churches, that occurs on the one soaking wet day of whichever month it is held in. Probably devised by God to remind us that, although in the Old Testament he promised not to flood the whole world again when people are least expecting it, he never said anything about Epsom or Milton Keynes.

Fig tree: fruit bearing tree that might justifiably feel slightly resentful about its role in Scripture, as it is remembered chiefly for covering the nakedness of

Adam and Eve after they sinned, and being cursed by Jesus so that he could make a preaching point.

Fish: symbol of the Christian church, possibly because fish are nervous creatures that stay well out of sight, and flop around helplessly when removed from their very limited environment.

Flee from the wrath that is to come: (1) follow Jesus (2) go on following Jesus (3) why have you stopped following Jesus? (4) get out of the bedroom before your four-year-old daughter wakes up and discovers what your seven-year-old son has done to her favourite toy in all the world.

Flower rota: hit-list compiled by Anglican mafia group that rules the flower arranging side of the Church of England operation with an iron hand. One or two of those brave or foolish enough to stand up to them have been known to wake in the morning to find the stalkless head of a favourite camellia under the duvet at the foot of their beds.

Food: that which builds us up and makes us strong. Jesus told his disciples in the fourth chapter of John's gospel that his food was to do the will of his Father in heaven. Doesn't sound too attractive as a regular diet, but experience suggests that steak and chips and apple pie taste even better when we are doing what we are told (See also **Obedience**).

Forgiveness: (1) something that, like most of the wonderful gifts of God, you are not allowed to receive unless you have already given it away (2) anagram of 'serving foes.'

Fraudulent teaching: (1) teaching that says you can't do it, only God can do it, and then when you find you can't do it, says it's your fault (2) teaching that ignores Jesus' teaching about cost, and offers conversion as though it was like a Debenhams store-card; one small, effortless prayer as a deposit and you can take as much as you want (3) teaching that says Christianity is not about formulae and goes on to make sure you have learned that principle word for word.

Freedom: a by-product of truth, and something many of us claim to desire more than anything. Only when it is actually offered, however, do we find out how much we actually want it, as the prisoner in the following dialogue discovers:

PRISONER: (*Loudly and passionately*) Help! Help! Someone help me! Help! Help! Someone has to help me get out of here! (*Etc.*)
RESCUER: (*Armed with a large key*) It's okay! Look! I've got a key. I can let you out
P: (*After looking at his watch*) Mmm. Actually, it's very nearly lunchtime, and the food really is not at all bad here. If you came back around, say, half two?
R: (*Indicates the bag he's carrying*) I've got plenty of food for both of us. Come on! Let's get going!
P: Oh. Err, right. Okay. Right! I'll just get my stuff together.
R: (*Looking around*) Stuff? What stuff? You haven't got any stuff: Come on, let's go!
P: Right. Right. You know, it's a bit chilly at this time of day. Maybe we'd be better to go in the morning after the sun has had a chance to –

R: (*Holding out a thick coat*) Here's a coat. Go on, put it on!
P: (*After putting the coat on*) Phew! It's going to be a bit jolly warm with this on. I'm already sweating and –
R: (*Impatiently offering his own coat*) Swap with me, for goodness sake! Mine's thinner. Now, let's get going before it's too late! Come on! (*They swop*)
P: Right! (*Hesitates*) You do know the way, do you?
R: (*Holds up a map*) I've got a map! I know the way!
P: Right! Right! Right! Right! Right . . .
R: Well, come on, then!
P: (*After a pause*) Look, I suppose you don't fancy moving in here with me instead, do you? It's really not that bad when you get used to it and every other Wednesday they put on a rather good sort of . . .
R: No, of course I don't fancy moving in with you! (*Beat*) Look – do you want to be free or not?
P: (*Rather sulkily*) Well, yes, but I think I ought to be the one to choose when I go. It doesn't seem fair to me that you just come barging in here without even making an appointment and –
R: But you were shouting about wanting to get out! I heard you! Now, come on! (*Grabs his arm*) Let's get –
P: Help! Help! I'm being kidnapped! Somebody help me! Help! Help! Rescue me! Help!
R: (*In disgust*) Oh, stay there then! (*Disappears*)
P: (*After a pause to make sure he's gone*) Help! Help! Somebody rescue me! Somebody has to get me out of here! Help! Help! (*Etc.*)

Frothy coffee: common evangelistic tool back in sixties and seventies together with table tennis and jolly group games. Now replaced by Coca-Cola and a space in which to be liberal and morose.

Fun: term for a sub-species of happiness. Over-used in the church, particularly by leaders of youth groups, who employ it to distinguish certain pleasurable but anaemic types of behaviour from certain other types of behaviour. As in:

> 'Good, well, we've had our fun time, now let's move on to prayer.'

Fundamentalist: (1) one who strictly maintains traditional Protestant beliefs such as the inerrancy of Scripture and literal acceptance of the creeds as fundamentals of Christianity (2) anagram of 'I'm a stunted flan' and 'snail fed mutant.'

Funeral: (1) an opportunity for wild rejoicing according to some Christians. You can see their point, of course. Being deprived of the company of someone you love is such a wonderful experience that it's hard to keep your feet from dancing (2) anagram of 'real fun.'

GATES OF HEAVEN

G

Gambling: vice generally held to be disapproved of by God, but to my certain knowledge there are places where you can get 10-1 against that turning out to be the case when we get to heaven, with 10 per cent of all winnings going to the book.

Garments: said Eli, 'High priests? I resent 'em!
They've torn all these garments I lent 'em
It would have cost more
If it hadn't been for
The fact that, like them, I just rent 'em.

Gates of heaven: improbable location, outside of which, according to one of the songs we used to sing at the back of the coach on the way to rugby matches, we are likely to find disconsolate, overweight Girl Guides, cars belonging to Religious Education teachers, Sabre jets and Playtex bras. This is because (as far as I can remember) the pearly gates just ain't that wide, the teacher's car won't get that far, the Lord ain't built no runways yet and Playtex bras won't stretch that far.

My friend Liz Pierce (you met her in the introduction) gets rather worried about the welcome she might expect at the entrance to heaven one day. I don't think she has any cause for concern. This is how I imagine it will be:

Slowly, uncertainly, Liz approaches the gates of heaven. Jesus is leaning against one of the gateposts, a little smile playing around his lips. Something that looks like a bulging supermarket carrier bag is hanging from one hand.

'Hello, Liz,' he says quietly.

'Oh, dear!' says Liz, hardly daring to meet his eyes, 'I'm afraid I don't deserve to be here at all.'

'Quite right,' says Jesus, 'but then nobody does, do they? That's not a problem, though. I've sorted that one out, remember?'

She stares at him for a moment before speaking again.

'Ah! No, of course not. I mean – of course! Thank you so much! What I meant was – I mean – well, what I meant was that I never really did anything . . . '

'Oh' says Jesus looking a little puzzled. 'What are all these, then?'

He holds the carrier bag out with both hands, open so that she can see the contents. She rifles through them. To her astonishment, inside are all the cards of encouragement and condolence and celebration that she sent to all sorts of people over the years.

'Some other person with the same name?' asks Jesus. His expression appears to be one of confusion, but the smile is still there in his eyes.

'Oh,' says Liz, 'well, yes, I suppose I sent them, but that's all.'

'Hmm.' Jesus closes the bag and puts it down beside him, just inside the gates. 'I know you're not coming in, but just poke your head round and take a look at this.'

Tentatively, she takes a few steps forward and nervously peers around the nearest gatepost. Immediately she gasps as she is overwhelmed by a sea of colour.

'Goodness me, what a marvellous garden!' she cries. 'Where on earth did all these wonderful flowers come from?'

'From you,' says Jesus, still leaning on the gatepost, 'these are all the flowers you gave me over the years.'

'Flowers I gave you?' she protests, 'I thought I gave them to – well, to people.'

'Look,' says Jesus, 'I don't want to go all technical and theological on you, but the way it works is that every time you gave, say, a bunch of tulips to Fred in hospital, the same bunch came straight up here to me. And I planted them. I've been having a great time. They grow here even if they've been cut. Do you like the garden you gave me?'

Liz is overwhelmed, and might argue if she wasn't so sure that she would lose the argument.

'I did get very impatient and grumpy and a bit resentful sometimes,' she says in a very small voice.

'True,' says Jesus, 'but usually only with your husband, and that gave him a chance to show his saintliness – sometimes. Oh! There's something else I wanted to show you.'

By now she has taken a few steps into heaven without realising it. Jesus moves over to a little stone table at the edge of the path, and picks up a heavy, leather-bound book. He thumbs through it in silence, stopping to read little bits from time to time.

'Err, what is that?' she asks at last.

Jesus looks up. 'This? Oh, it's just a record of all the chats and conversations you had with people when you visited them in hospital and met them on buses and in the street, and – oh, all over the place. Some good ones here. Thank you. You really cheered me up sometimes. And you filled in quite a few gaps in the road for all sorts of people. I'm not saying you were perfect, but you had a jolly good go at doing things for me. Well done.'

She is in tears. It's all too much. Jesus puts his arm around her and leads her away through the flowers. The air is fragrant with the scents of early summer.

'Come on, Liz,' he says gently, 'I've got lots more things to show you, and there's someone I really want you to meet.'

She looks up suddenly and says through her sniffles. 'Do you know. I feel awfully well.'

'Of course you do,' he replies, smiling broadly now, 'you've come home.'

Gender: crucial contemporary issue in the field of Bible publication. God must be kicking himself for so carelessly selecting a time and place for his visit to the world in which male and female roles were quite so rigidly and unequally defined. Preoccupation with gender issues is moving us inexorably towards such monstrosities as 'the word became androgynous flesh.'

General Booth: (1) celebrated founder of the Salvation Army, and not, as some have foolishly supposed, the inventor of the public phone box.

Getting into small groups: (1) something very few people actually want to do, but everyone dismally agrees to co-operate with because they suppose that, somewhere in the divine scheme of things, it must make sense (2) obsessional ploy of guest speakers at weekends away, particularly those who are afraid they haven't got ninety minutes worth of material.

Girding up your loins: not altogether sure, but pending reliable definitions it seems safe to assume that this is something best done in the privacy of one's own home.

Girgashites: (1) a tribe mentioned in the Old Testament books of Genesis, Deuteronomy, Joshua, 1 Chronicles and Nehemiah (2) sounds like some appallingly volcanic gastric complaint, as in: 'I've been in bed for the last week with a bad case of the girgashites.'

Gittite: (1) member of a tribe mentioned in 2 Samuel and 1 Chronicles (2) phonetic expression of what Prince Charles says when angrily dismissing a servant who has displeased him.

Give God a round of applause!: a suggestion occasionally made by worship leaders to congregations. Not entirely clear how God reacts to being treated like a Friday night performance of *The Mousetrap*, but one supposes he must get used to these things.

Gnostic: (1) Christian heretic of the first to third centuries claiming to have knowledge of spiritual mysteries (2) agnostic without a.

Go in peace: (1) injunction to the congregation at the close of the Anglican Communion service (2) something that is only possible for those blessed with an en suite bathroom and toilet.

Gob smacked: what Saint Paul was, literally and figuratively, in the early part of the twenty-third chapter of Acts.

God of Gods, Lord of Lords: (1) the source of peace and grace (2) W.G. Grace.

God of the gaps: divine, caring presence all over the world and especially on London underground stations.

God told me: a spiritual half-nelson. Widely used, in particular, by those who have not been told anything by God but wish to influence others.

Godsend: (2) unexpected but very necessary and welcome event or acquisition (2) best left to him while we look after ours.

Goliath: (1) a warning to modern youth, this Philistine giant died as a result of getting stoned, and all it took was a couple of rocks (2) known as Goliath of Gath, although recent research suggests that his real name may well have been Golias of Gas, the confusion being caused by the fact that, as with more modern combatants such as Mike Tyson and Chris Eubank, he spoke with a lisp, and was far too big to argue with.

Gone, gone, gone, gone, yes my sins are gone: (1) a fine sentiment embodying the crux of the gospel message (2) possibly the most annoying song in the entire history of terminally annoying songs. Perhaps it should be rewritten in the following form:

> Gone, gone, gone, gone
> Yes, every jot of musical discrimination
> I ever had is gone
> Of all the choruses we sing I hate this one
> Rip it out of Mission Praise
> Shred it with some mayonnaise
> Feed it to the goat until the da-a-a-amn thing's gone.

A B C D E F G H I J K L M N O P Q R S T U V W X Y Z

A B C D E F G H I J K L M N O P Q R S T U V W X Y Z

Good news: inexplicable to the vast majority of people because no one has helped them to understand about the bad news. If the current tendency to dilute or deny the bad news continues, there will be little point in telling people that the good news will save them. Their next, eminently reasonable question will be, 'Saved from what?' (See also **Hell**).

Good Samaritan: fictional biblical character in a parable told by Jesus. Claimed as a Tory by the Conservatives because his investments had provided sufficient resources for him to be able to help if he so wished, as a socialist by the Labour Party because he was actually willing to share his money, and by the Liberal Democrats because the crowd who were listening to the parable automatically assumed that he would be useless.

Gospel writers: Matthew, Mark, Luke and John. Serious historical and theological research strongly suggests that, contrary to popular tradition, it is extremely unlikely that any one of these four significant individuals went to bed with their trousers on.

Grace: prayer said before meals by most Christians when fellow believers are visiting, and by rather fewer when they are not.

Gratitude: quality not much in evidence among the Israelites after God miraculously provided food in the wilderness. Recorded comments include:

> 'Now, don't get me wrong, I do like God. There's just something about his manna . . . '

Grave error: dying without Jesus.

Greed: (1) unpleasant grasping tendency, in stark contrast with one's own balanced, restrained, rather modest and deeply spiritual approach to the acquisition of money and possessions (2) immeasurably more serious and more widespread sin in the Christian church than the ones people usually make such a fuss about.

Greenbelt: (1) Christian music festival which, in the good old days, was more or less an effluvial swamp with tents floating on top of it (2) amphibious judo qualification.

Grip: term used by some Christians in their salutation at the end of a letter, thus, 'Yours in his grip.' Suggests that God is in the habit of carrying his followers around in a small leather travelling case.

Guilt: illicit but powerful preaching aid, easily induced by Christian speakers when all other ploys have failed. Particularly effective with those among us who began our lives by apologising at length to the midwife for causing her so much trouble. Bearing this in mind, one popular chorus might be expressed in these words:

> The First World War
> The fire of London and the fall
> All down to me, to me
> For all your woes, in fact for anything at all
> Please feel free, to blame me
> Our guilt reigns, our guilt reigns
> Our guilt reigns, our guilt reigns.

HELLO-O-O

H

Habakkuk: (1) Old Testament prophet who asked God some very blunt questions and got some very big answers. Little substance in the claim that he has come back to life and will present a new religious cookery programme on television entitled *Ready, Steady, Habakkuk.*

Ham: second son of Noah. A less than perceptive lad, Ham never did catch on to the reason why, throughout the voyage of the ark, he was so nervously avoided by Mr and Mrs Pig.

Hands: useful things on the ends of our arms whose elevation relative to ground level in certain church circles has acquired a significance that is a little puzzling, to say the least. In this connection, one friend of mine was instructed by a group of local elders that prayer is properly conducted in the following manner.

First of all, she was told, the supplicants raise their arms as far as they will go, but with both hands bent at the wrists so that they are parallel with the ground. (Pay attention or you might miss out on learning how to pray!) Next, you walk around the edge of the room, pushing towards the floor with your flat hands in such a way that heaven is *pressed* down by the movement. What one does with the pile of heaven that must be accumulated in the middle of the room by this process was never explained.

Jesus has some interesting things to say about prayer in the sixth chapter of Matthew's gospel, but I seem to recall that his ideas were much simpler and saner than the things my friend was told. Still, he was only the Son of God. What would he know about prayer?

Hanging: much in favour with certain Christians who like to bathe daily in the deep end of the Old Testament and have no way of controlling the waves of violent compassion that engulf them at times.

Hanging gardens of Babylon: one of the seven ancient wonders of the world, situated in the country that enslaved Israel in Daniel's time. In our own impoverished age we are limited to an abandoned Millennium Dome and the hanging baskets of Basildon.

He's a lovely man: phrase used as moral justification for going on to list the deliciously fascinating ways in which the person in question is not lovely at all.

Healing: (1) something God always does (2) something God never does (3) something God sometimes does and sometimes doesn't do (4) something that is stubbornly resisted by sufferers who deliberately refuse to understand or join in with what the rest of their fellowship is trying to do.

Hearing from God: can be a confusing and slightly tricky business. Some people talk as though they are in the habit of having a chat with God over coffee every morning. 'I said this and he said that, and he pointed this out and I reminded him that . . . ' Books have been written that purport to include the exact words spoken by God to a particular individual, and whole movements and ministries have been based on specific revelations of one kind or another. The Bible suggests that God will certainly communicate very directly and clearly when he wants to, which makes it all the more disturbing on those occasions when the modern church proceeds on the basis of someone sort of feeling that the Lord might possibly be saying something or other. Perhaps we should be asking God for the kind of clear guidance that was given to Joseph two thousand years ago. Remember the thirteenth and fourteenth verses of the second chapter of Matthew's gospel?

> When they had gone, an angel of the Lord appeared to Joseph in a dream. 'Get up,' he said, 'take the child and his mother and escape to Egypt. Stay there until I tell you, for Herod

> is going to search for the child to kill him.' So he got up, took the child and his mother during the night and left for Egypt.

Pretty clear, direct and specific, don't you think? No wonder Joseph collected everybody together and upped and offed with such speed and alacrity in the middle of the night. No room for argument or debate. Horrid Herod was coming and that precious baby had to be kept safe. But suppose the message had not been as crystal clear as this. Suppose Joseph had gone to Bernard, his house-group leader (well, he might have had one, and they're all called Bernard) for advice, after having a sort of feeling that maybe God was saying that Egypt might possibly be the place to go. How might the conversation have developed?

BERNARD: Okay, Joe, mate, just take the weight off your feet and relax. Super to see you. Wife okay?
JOSEPH: Fine, yes.
B: Baby doing well?
J: Oh, smashing, thanks. Yes, both doing fine. Got some nice presents from some visitors the other day. Bit odd. The presents, I mean – well, the visitors as well, actually. But nice. Visitors and presents, all very nice.
B: Good! So, what's on your mind?
J: Right. Well, Bernard, it's just that I've been having this sort of feeling that – well, that maybe the Lord's trying to tell me that I ought to move to Egypt for a while.

B: (*staring insightfully, and after a short, nodding pause*) Uh-huh. Go on.
J: Well, that's more or less it, really. I've just got this kind of idea that God could be wanting the baby out of the way because of – of Herod and all that. As you can imagine, it's not an easy decision to make, and I wondered what you might think about it all.
B: (*slowly and thoughtfully*) First of all, Joe, I think what you're saying does make an awful lot of sense. Herod might come after the baby. Egypt's a long way away. Escape while you can and come back when it's safe. That's good logic. I can see exactly where you're coming from. (*Pause for silent arrow prayer*) Look, would it be all right if I were to ask you a few simple questions?
J: Yes, of course, fire away.
B: Well, first of all – Egypt.
J: Egypt.
B: (*nodding meaningfully*) Yes, Egypt. (*Leaning forward*) Joe, in which part of the world were our people enslaved before Moses thwarted Pharaoh and led us on a forty year trek through the wilderness into the Promised Land?
J: Er – well, that would be Egypt.
B: Exactly – Egypt! Joe, are you seriously trying to tell me that God supports the idea of that precious little boy and his family scuttling off *back* to Egypt just because there's a spot of trouble brewing in this part of his world, the Promised Land that was set apart for Abraham and his descendants all those centuries ago? Is the idea of doing that in any way honouring to

God? (*Leaning back with an impartial air*) But never mind what I think. You tell me how you see it.

J: (*shaking his head*) You know, I never thought of it like that. I guess you're right. No, it certainly wouldn't be Egypt, would it. I've obviously got that wrong. Thank you, Bernard. A very good point. Well, somewhere else, perhaps?

B: Hold on a moment. Another question. It's this, Joe. Your desire to escape – is it really about the baby, or is it more about you?

J: Well – I suppose it could be both really, if I'm honest. I'm not very keen on being murdered by Herod.

B: Okay, and if you clear off to some safe place with Mary and the baby, what is Herod going to do? Take your time. Think about it. What is this so-called king of ours likely to do?

J: Well, those Magi people aren't going to tell him where we are. They said so. They're going straight home without seeing Herod because they had a sort of feeling that the Lord might possibly be telling them that it wouldn't be a very good idea.

B: Right! And how is that going to make Herod feel?

J: Cross?

B: Mm.

J: Very cross?

B: Mmm.

J: Angry?

B: Mmmm!

J: Very angry indeed?

B: Mmmmm! Extremely angry, yes. Furious. And I think you know as well as I do, Joe, that the next item on his agenda will be the murder of just about every male child in Bethlehem, or at any rate, all those under the age of two or thereabouts. He's like that. That's his way of doing things. Am I right or am I wrong?
J: (*sighing*) You're right. You are so right.
B: Joe, do you honestly believe that God is going to allow all those innocent children to be killed just so that you can run away and hide in a little safe corner somewhere? Is that the mark of the God we worship? Is it, Joe?
J: (*solemnly*) No, Bernard, it is not.
B: Joe, you believe that our God is a God of miracles, don't you?
J: Oh, yes, I know he is.
B: Okay, well consider this. Maybe the answer is that you go openly to Herod with the baby and declare that he is the Son of God. Joe, do you believe that the Lord, the Creator of the universe, is capable of protecting you in that situation? Have you the strength and the faith and the courage to rely on his power instead of running away and risking the lives of others?
J: (*fired up*) Yes! Yes! That is exactly what I'm going to do! Bernard, I can't thank you enough for helping me to see things so much more clearly. (*Stands*) I'm going straight home to tell Mary what we've been talking about. She's got a very level head. I'm sure she'll agree with what I've decided. Thank goodness I came to see you, Bernard. (*Shakes head in wonder*) Gosh! The future

of the whole world may well depend on this one decision. When I think how close I came to getting it wrong . . .

Heavenly host: (1) a large assembly of those who inhabit heaven, such as angels (2) one who puts a glass and a whiskey decanter by your elbow when you arrive and leaves it there until you depart.

Heavy Shepherding: usually results in sheep getting squashed.

Hebrews: (1) nineteenth book of the New Testament, possibly written by Paul (2) description of the primary function of the office junior.

Heel-bouncing: a phenomenon that often accompanies violent prayer by smartly suited Christian executives involved in an organisation ending with the letters 'MFI', when they form a rugby scrum around visiting speakers before they deliver their talks.

Helium industry: what someone mistakenly thought I said on being asked the direction in which I would like my Christian life to go. As I had actually indicated that I would like to be involved in a 'healing ministry', the conversation that followed was confused, to say the least. Quite warmed to the idea after a while, actually. A constant supply of helium could be useful in certain circumstances (See also **Divine Crescendo**).

Hell: (1) place of eternal unhappiness for those who have decided to refuse God's invitation to come home to him (2) a concept that has been denied or significantly diluted by many modern teachers and theologians. Before getting too excited about such cheerily optimistic views, it might be as well to check with God that he actually goes along with them. The Creator of the universe can be very slow and (let's be brutally honest) a little dense when it comes to staying *au fait* with new and exciting theological advances (See also **Good News**).

Hello-o-o!: often accompanied by a hand cupped behind one ear, this device is used by some Christian speakers at strategic points in their talks to signal that their listeners are not sufficiently awake in mind or spirit to hear and agree with what has just been said.

Helmet of salvation: part of Paul's 'whole armour of God' as mentioned in Ephesians. A challenging concept for those of us who still can't seem to find a way to remove the Y-fronts of weariness and the balaclava of bewilderment.

Here am I, Lord: send him, or possibly her, or – anyone else, really.

Here's a question for you all: phrase generally used by one leading or teaching a group, especially in churches where spontaneity is very carefully organised. Actually means: 'I'm going to tell you something, but I'm quite happy for each of you to wriggle like a butterfly on a pin for a minute or two while you worry about whether or not you know the right answer.'

Heresy: (1) belief contrary to orthodox doctrine (2) artificially constructed in-house singing group auditioned and selected by the Spanish Inquisition. Exposure to their performances was the final, terrible threat to those who refused to recant.

Herod Antipas: (1) rich, powerful ruler over the Jews from 4 BC–AD 9, who had everything he wanted handed to him on a plate.

Holes: things in our lives that we all fall through at one time or another. Can be family or finance or health or church or friendship. Spiralling helplessly down is not much fun, to say the least, but experience suggests there will ultimately be a place where we find our feet once more. Or, to put it another way:

> When you fall through the holes in your life,
> Don't think it surprising or odd,
> Be glad that it's planned, you will finally land,
> On the solid forgiveness of God.

Holistic healing: (1) healing in which the whole person is treated, and not just the symptoms of an ailment (2) spiritual healing in which the sufferer is not actually healed of their ailment, but it doesn't seem to matter because some very serious and satisfactory nodding happens.

Holy ground: (1) area around the Burning Bush (2) brand of coffee we shall all drink in heaven (3) Old Trafford (4) Lords.

Hosea: rollercoaster of an Old Testament book about a prophet who went through much inconvenience and pain in order to be obedient. When he asked God if he could avoid the inconvenience and pain and still be a prophet, the reply was, 'No wayer, Hosea!'

Hospitality: virtue encouraged by Jesus, who said we should invite people who are not our friends as much or more so than those who are. Fine unless we all start doing it, in which case any invitation to dinner will be regarded with deep suspicion. 'Come to dinner at your house? Oh, so that's what you think of us, is it?'

House Church: (1) church that meets in a school (2) church that meets in a factory (3) church that meets in a theatre (4) church that meets in a shed (5) church that meets on a bouncy castle.

House Church football teams: have tended to do badly in tournaments for three reasons (a) continually moving the goalposts (b) playing with their arms in the air and their eyes shut (c) marching around the edge of the pitch claiming victory for the Lord when they should be playing.

Hugging: very fashionable in the modern church. For decency's sake, has to be executed in such a fashion that a garden fence and two eighteen inch flowerbeds could be inserted between the feet of the two people who are hugging. Back patting should be avoided as it looks too much like a mutual bringing up of wind.

Human beings: the main reason for God sending his Son, and, coincidentally and ridiculously, the main obstacle to the fulfilment of his plan.

A B C D E F G H I J K L M N O P Q R S T U V W X Y Z

I

I cannot tell: (1) what bank clerks say when they phone in sick (2) title of a stirring hymn set to the tune of *Danny Boy*. Might be reconstructed using the following words to express the feelings of someone who has been taken to a charismatic service without any preparation or warning:

I cannot tell why I allowed my sister
To drag me here to this benighted place.
Or why my neighbour's speaking Esperanto
With such a weird expression on his face.
But this I know, if that mad preacher picks on me
I shall insert his hand-held microphone
Into a place where all is pain and darkness
And that will be my cue to leave the twilight zone.

I love you in the Lord: phrase that describes the spiritual bond between all believers, but all too often means 'as a person I find nothing in you to attract me at all, but in the purely statutory sense I have to accept that there must be some kind of spiritual bond between us.'

I sense that we ought to move into prayer over this: I've run out of arguments. Just give me a few moments breathing space and I'm sure I'll come up with something to bring you round to my way of thinking.

I suddenly really sense the presence of the Lord in this church: God was not able to get there for the beginning of the service, but he's just this moment turned up, so the service can get going now.

I will thoroughly purge away your dross: generous offer by the prophet Isaiah in the first chapter of his book to undertake radical colonic irrigation for the constipated ones of Israel.

Icon: (1) a devotional painting or carving, usually on wood, of Christ or another holy figure (2) it is not generally known that, as a creative race, icon artists are less than confident. When addressing them on the subject of their art, one should look very directly into their faces and express one's response to their work with delicacy and subtlety. This is known in artistic circles as icon-tact.

Illuminated manuscripts: mediaeval invention that allowed monks to read in bed.

Immersion: the lowering of the whole person into water during the sacrament of baptism. As with witches and eggs, the floaters are rejected.

Impatience: symptoms of this vice are frequently visible in church services. Those who sneak a glance at their watches as yet another hymn begins may wish that they could sing the following words instead of the traditional version:

Dear Lord and Father of mankind
It's twenty five to one
So please be brief, our joint of beef
Will burn and shrink because I think
I've left the oven on, I've left the oven on.

Impious: (1) profane (2) invoices issued by elves.

Impoliteness: major sin in old-fashioned Anglican circles, almost (but not quite) on a par with sitting in someone else's pew.

In a very real sense: subtle phrase frequently employed in Christian circles, and usually applied to doubtful propositions. Frequently means 'not in the slightest.'

In fellowship: what Christians are because they have Jesus in common.

Amazingly, the second best market for my books is Germany. 'Germans have no sense of humour,' declared a humourless English friend, when it was first suggested that my books should be translated into that language, adding with dry, unconscious humour, 'and German Christians have even less.'

He was wrong. German Christians have a fine sense of humour, and are happy to express it as soon as they are given permission to do so.

Knowing this, there is always a temptation for someone like me to push the boundaries beyond acceptable limits. Flippant references to two World Wars might be something to avoid, for instance. But even this tender topic pales to insignificance compared with an issue that truly does touch the hearts of millions of German people. I am speaking of football.

As we all know, a recording that is regularly repeated in this country features Geoff Hurst achieving his hat-trick during extra time to bring England victory over West Germany in the final of the 1966 World Cup.

'They think it's all over!' yells the near hysterical commentator as crowds swarm onto the pitch seconds before Hurst's goal is scored, then, as the ball hits the back of the net, 'It is now!'

We fed on that moment for years, didn't we? Well, we had to. The next four decades saw Germany achieve many footballing honours, while England won very little. Then, in September 2001, England played Germany in a lead-up match to the 2002 World Cup, and I began a tour of that beautiful country two days later.

Perhaps it was insensitive of me, but what an opportunity! Each evening I held up my left hand with four fingers and one thumb extended,

A B C D E F G H I J K L M N O P Q R S T U V W X Y Z

followed by my right hand with just the index finger showing.

Five–one, I intoned with sinful relish. 'Five goals to one. We scored five goals, and you scored one. Put another way, we won the match because we scored more goals than you, four more to be exact, and you lost. You see, you only managed to score one, whereas we scored – let me see, what was it? Oh, yes, of course, I remember now. We scored five, didn't we? Four more than you, in fact.'

Translation was unnecessary. Everyone got the point. The response? Low growling, giggles, a few jeers and one or two shouts of objection. All of it, including the growling, was done in a good spirit, though. We all laughed in the end. We were bound to because the bond between those German people and me was more permanent than anything to do with supporting the same team or even sharing the same nationality. We were all followers of Jesus. This means that when the real battles come, we shall unhesitatingly line up on the same side. We are brothers and sisters.

That is what it should all be about. Competition is great. Football is wonderful. Differences in background, culture and individual experience are to be appreciated and enjoyed. In the final analysis, though, the Spirit that draws us together is greater than anything that keeps us apart.

In these times: silly, pompous, Christian speaker's way of saying 'nowadays.'

In your arms I would lay: line in a Christian song expressing the feelings of a chicken that is lovesick, and therefore egg-bound.

Incarnation: (1) the embodiment of God the Son in human flesh as Jesus Christ (2) this country, as illustrated by what happens on the M25 at most times, on most days.

Incense: (1) a gum or spice producing a sweet smell when burned in religious ceremonials (2) not to be confused with a similar word that has a very different meaning, as exemplified by the militantly low-church lady who refused to enter her local High Anglican church, saying, 'You won't get me in there – I can smell incest a mile off . . . '

Inconsistencies in the Bible: attacked by those who wish to discredit the authenticity of Scripture, defended by those who are less than secure about the authenticity of Scripture, and celebrated by those who see glorious and reassuring reality and authenticity where others see only inconsistency.

Indissolubilists: excellently lumpy, unattractive and pedantic name for those who believe that the church should never agree to remarry divorcees. Indisswhateveritists are almost invariably not drawn from the ranks of the divorced.

Ineffable: (1) impossible to express in words (2) cannot be sworn about.

A B C D E F G H I J K L M N O P Q R S T U V W X Y Z

Infidel: (1) an adherent to a religion other than Christianity (2) where the contents of Cuba's president are located.

Infinity: (1) the state of being boundless (2) the last half hour of something one really hates (3) the half hour immediately before something one is really looking forward to (4) any lifeless church service (5) Scottish television on New Year's Eve.

Inflexible expectation: one of the major barriers to communication, not just in the church, but in most other areas of life as well. One thing that God and other people have in common is that, whatever we may think, they are always capable of producing a surprise. A fact that the couple in this dialogue have yet to learn:

A: Ah, thank goodness you're back. And did you – ?
B: Yes, I did. I went to see –
A: Right! And did he – ?
B: No, I'm afraid he didn't. I know you were hoping that –
A: Yes, I was. So, there's no point in – ?
B: None at all, I'm afraid. Not even if –
A: Really? Not even then? So did he not even consider – ?
B: Not ever. Not once. And so we have to face the fact that –
A: I know. I so hoped that –
B: I know you did. If only I hadn't –
A: Well, you did try not to! But the weather all that summer was –
B: True. That's true. And you'd just been through –

A: Yes, I had. Do you remember that night, the night when we sat and all we did was – ?
B: Several times. And I recall us saying that we would always –
A: Gosh, I'd forgotten. We did, didn't we? And now I guess we have to face the fact that he's going to end up in –
B: Right! How could he be so different from – ?
A: Oh it's a puzzle. I guess he'll just have to stay in prison until he's –
B: Finished his sentence?

Inner peace: like a bicycle's inner tube. You hardly notice it when it's working properly; you get very uncomfortable when it isn't, it has to be repaired from time to time, and if it doesn't get renewed when it wears out, you won't make any progress at all.

Innkeeper: first century hotelier with no spare rooms who can nevertheless claim to be responsible for the fact that Jesus was fortunate enough to spend the very earliest part of his life in a stable environment.

Innovation: (1) bringing in new, untried methods (2) guitar played in a pub.

Isaac: son of Abraham and father of Jacob and Esau. Abraham's experience with Isaac as a boy is a vivid illustration of the fact that, if you are going to be a parent, you have to be willing to make sacrifices.

Isaiah: (1) a major Old Testament prophet, probably a little like David Pawson in drag (2) sounds like a helpful personal motto for aspirately challenged men

A B C D E F G H I J K L M N O P Q R S T U V W X Y Z

to repeat to themselves when confronted with plunging necklines.

Israel: the people of God. Actually means 'he struggles (or wrestles) with God.' Fortunately, instead of three falls, two submissions or a knockout, all each of us has to worry about in our confrontation with Big Daddy is one fall, one submission and a redemption.

It depends what you mean by healing: strange, coy response from those involved with healing ministries where nothing ever happens, when asked if they have actually seen anybody healed. The assumption that someone with a bad leg might, as a result of prayer, no longer have a bad leg, appears to be too naïve and simplistic to count for much (see also: **Healing**, **Holistic healing**, and **Kerin, Dorothy**).

It must therefore be perfectly clear to the simplest among us that . . . : phrase used by some Christian speakers and writers immediately prior to launching into wild and unfounded speculation.

JOT AND TITTLE

J

Jacob's ladder: probably the – oh, so vexing! – result of catching his tights while he was wrestling with the angel.

Jael: wife of Heber, this lady nailed Sisera's head to the ground with a tent peg, thus adding fuel to the argument of those who say that the practical side of camping should be left to men.

Jail: a place known to many Christians over the years. Saint Paul, for instance, spent more time behind bars than an Australian backpacker.

James: New Testament book that any reasonable person must believe God should never have allowed into the canon. Full of references to doing things as well as believing. Two quite amusing jokes as well. Ridiculous definition of true religion in chapter one, verse twenty-seven. It is thought James may have been the brother of Jesus. I rest my case.

Janus: mythical god of doors and beginnings, who could look forwards and backwards at the same time because he had two faces. Would have been ideally suited to involvement in a number of modern Christian businesses.

Jargon: language or terms restricted to a particular group or culture, including the Christian one. Personally, I think the Lord would have us cry out mightily against such abominations.

Jawbone of an ass: weapon employed by Samson in the book of Judges, and by many a preacher and political spokesperson in this age (See also **Samson**).

Jehovah's Witnesses: a millenarian Christian sect whose members appear to believe, inexplicably, that for the limited number of God's elect, eternal life will bear a close resemblance to suburban middle-class England in the fifties.

Jesus: (1) Saviour of the world who has made it possible for prodigals to go home and find out how much they are loved (2) Passionately Resolutely Insists On Radically Improving Tomorrow's Yesterday.

Jesus really shone out from his face: comment occasionally made by people who have encountered an individual, often in wretched, problem-filled circumstances, who seems to radiate the love of Christ in a way that is rarely encountered in day-to-day life.

Always good to hear, but the fact is that the vast majority of Christians, myself included, do not usually manage more than a slight glow at the best of times. I suppose it gives us all something to aim at, but our spiritual self-confidence can be somewhat eroded when we compare ourselves with the shiny person in question. How come Jesus shines out from them and not from me? Is it because I haven't tried hard enough? Are there terrible sins I haven't got round to confessing? Is it easier to have Jesus shining out from your face when you live in Africa or Bangladesh than when you spend most of your time in Luton or Durham or Hailsham?

I guess the resolution of all this might lie in our growing awareness that the place where we are as individuals is of little importance compared with the body of Christ as a whole. That person who seems to project the love of Jesus so effortlessly is a part of me, just as I am a part of them. Their smile is my smile. My low wattage glow is their low wattage glow. Do I dare to own whatever I find, good or bad, in my brothers and sisters? Do they dare the same? Am I prepared to laugh and weep with them, no matter what may be happening in me? The affirmative answer given to that question by Christians in the past has already changed the world. My contribution, small as it might be, will continue that crucial process.

Jimmy Swaggart: (1) American evangelist shamed by public exposure of his sin (2) anagram of 'gag my trim jaws.'

Job: (1) unfortunate but ultimately justified Old Testament character who, because of a deal made between God and the devil, found his life was breaking down into three main phases: pre-boil, boil and post-boil (2) it appears that Job had problems with the Creator on the football field as well. In the eighth verse of chapter 19 he speaks of God's defensive skills:

'He has blocked my way so I cannot pass . . . '

Earlier, in the eleventh verse of chapter nine, he refers to the sparkling, George Best-like quality of God's attacking play:

'He performs wonders that cannot be fathomed, miracles that cannot be counted. When he passes me I cannot see him; when he goes by, I cannot perceive him . . . '

Jonah (see Joppa): reluctant prophet who had to learn to be grateful for everything, good or bad, that God gave him, as when he emerged from the belly of the giant fish covered in goo, and said:
'Thank you. Lord, when you rebuke us,
With your gift of whale mucus.'

Joppa (see Jonah): Jonah took ship out of Joppa,
By telling the captain a whopper,
But after the storm, God said, 'He'll reform,
The man's come a whale of a cropper.'

Jot: one half of a very popular Old Testament comedy duo. Never quite as funny on his own as he was when appearing with Tittle (See also **Tittle**).

Jude: (1) writer of the twenty-sixth, penultimate book of the New Testament, which concludes with a reassurance for those who do not wish to be slain in the Spirit: 'Now, unto him who is able to keep you from falling . . . ' (2) person who got Paul McCartney worked up to a point of screaming hysteria, due, as far as one can tell, to the possibility that they might let him down.

Judea: (1) Greek and Roman name for Judah, usually refers to the southern part of the country, sometimes used for the whole land, including Galilee and Samaria (2) what Jude says when answering the phone to Paul McCartney, always assuming Paul still speaks to him after being let down so badly.

Judge not that you be not judged: important feature of the teaching of Jesus, and one that a couple of people I could name would be well advised to take on board before it's too late.

It really is so easy and sometimes enjoyable to judge the behaviour of others.

Some years ago, during one of those long lazy lunches that are so enjoyable when work is waiting to be done, a friend described a singular experience that had affected him deeply. His account affected me deeply as well, and the memory has rattled around disturbingly in my head ever since. Only recently have I worked out what I really think about it.

Now, before continuing I should warn you frankly that what you are about to hear is, on the face of it, a tale of sacrilege, set in a lavatorial context. If this grim fact dissuades you from reading any further I shall understand. Please feel free to turn your attention to something else as soon as you reach the full stop at the end of this paragraph.

Still reading? Okay, but I did warn you . . .

My friend went to one of those big evangelistic rallies where a famous speaker is imported to address Christians from local churches, together with those they have dragged along to be converted – sorry, I mean those they have invited along to hear the gospel. This meeting happened in my friend's church, a large building with excellent modern facilities, including toilets leading off from the foyer space just inside the main door. The place was packed, the air filled with a buzz of excitement and anticipation that dwindled to a profound hush as the speaker took his place at the microphone.

He was good – no doubt about that. My friend, who was seated at the end of one of the long front pews, was genuinely moved and entertained by the first half of the evening. The combination of deep, uncompromising holiness, masterful delivery and finely honed story-telling was powerful. Apart from anything else, the man looked so impressive. The fine head of waved, iron-grey hair, the discreet, perfectly fitting suit and the highly polished, stylish brown brogues all spoke of a man at ease with God, himself and the rest of the world.

After forty-five minutes there was an interval. The audience, thrilled with an infusion of borrowed assurance, buzzed excitedly once more as they left their seats to seek (in increasing order of possible availability) toilets, teas and an opportunity to spend money on the speaker's books.

My friend knew the church well. Toilet queues in the foyer were sure to be endless. Slipping quietly through the side door near his seat at the end of the pew, he hurried down a corridor past the vestry and the church office, turned a corner and passed through a swing-door into the little toilet block reserved for those involved in services or presentations.

It was while he was sitting in one of the two cubicles a few moments later that he heard someone else come into the block, and saw, through the six-inch gap at the bottom of the cubicle door, a pair of shining brown brogues moving in the direction of the urinals. The great man was about to relieve himself.

My friend tried to pretend that he didn't exist.

He then heard two things. One was quite predictable and need not concern us here. The other was a deep inhalation of breath and a long outward sigh of satisfaction and relief on which the words: 'Je-e-e-sus Christ!' were conveyed with all the passion of a mystic at prayer.

This moment was the climax of my friend's story, and I understood why the experience had been a disturbing one. The man who had exuded holiness and self-control on that platform just now was not the same man who had uttered what sounded to my friend's ears like blatant profanity in the gents' toilet a few moments later.

A B C D E F G H I J K L M N O P Q R S T U V W X Y Z

My reaction to this story on the spot, and for a long time afterwards, was one of disappointment and cynicism. Here was yet another example of that depressingly common gap between the public and private faces of Christianity. The public one was just a beautifully polished act, an accomplished piece of outward role-playing to cover and conceal the spiritual vacuum that existed within. The voice, the hair, the suit, the stories – all meaningless show. Perhaps he believed nothing at all.

This ridiculously narrow and condemning attitude persisted until I happened to catch my own mouth muttering something unspeakable in a particular situation, and simple justice forced me to ask myself if I considered the work I did to be rendered null and void as a result. I felt so ashamed. What right had I to judge one of my brothers who was struggling to reach people in the way that seemed right to him? Had I not always argued that Christianity is a ragged, difficult thing, only able to work if we allow the Spirit of God to inhabit our relationships and our attitudes to each other?

When God alone is with us in the strange, trackless forests of what we really are, there is potential for us to do or say all sorts of unpleasant things. Take heart. Whatever those things might be, he will forgive us, as long as we extend the same courtesy to others.

Just: oddly ubiquitous and slightly annoying word in extempore Christian prayer. In fact, I just sense we should just pray about it now. Lord, we just ask that this word will just drop out of usage and that we will just replace it just with something that just makes more sense . . .

Justice: (1) the exercise of God's authority in the maintenance of right (2) no lemon.

Justification: (1) function of word processors that makes sure everything is tidied up satisfactorily at the end of the line (2) divine, grace-filled initiative that makes sure everything is tidied up at the end of the line.

KATYDID

K

Katydid: creature mentioned in the twenty-second verse of the eleventh chapter of Leviticus, this was one of the insects that God allowed the Israelites to eat. Soon to be featured in a life-cycle documentary in two parts, entitled 'What the Katydid did' and 'What the Katydid did next'.

Keeping your temper: very valuable at times. Politeness is one of the most attractive qualities a human being can have. It is also one of the greatest barriers to progress in the Christian church. Imagine if Jesus had said to the Pharisees, 'Err, excuse me, I hope you'll forgive me for saying this, but I do think you are just a little bit viperish. I mean, gosh, we all have trouble in that area, but I think you might have a special problem . . . ' At its worse the disease of over-politeness and good temper at all costs can result in something like the following dialogue:

A: Look, can I say something to you?
B: Yes, of course.
A: Well, I think we ought to clear the air about what happened the other day. I just want to say how sorry I am for what I said.
B: Oh, well, no, I'm sorry for putting you in a position where you felt the need to apologise for what you said.
A: That's very nice of you, but look, I'm really sorry for putting you in a position where you felt the need to apologise for putting me in a position where I had to apologise for what I said.
B: Oh, good heavens, no, I'm just sorry for putting you in a position where you felt the need to apologise when I felt the need to apologise for putting you in a position where you felt you had to apologise for what you said.
A: Well, that's great, but I really want to say how sorry I am that you felt the need to apologise for putting me in a position where I felt the need to apologise for putting you in a position where you felt the need to apologise for putting me in a position where I felt I had to apologise for what I said.
B: Oh, no, I'm just sorry that I put you in a position where –

A: What did I say?
B: What do you mean 'What did I say?'
A: What do you mean 'What do you mean "What did I say"'?
B: Well, I don't know what you mean when you ask 'What do you mean "What do you mean 'What did I say?'" You must remember what you said. You just apologised for saying it.
A: Yes, but you said you were sorry for putting me in a position where I felt the need to apologise for what I'd said.
B: Well, yes, but that was before you told me you've forgotten what you said. If you hadn't forgotten what you said I'd still be sorry for putting you in a position where you felt the need to apologise for –
A: I've remembered!
B: Remembered what?
A: I've remembered what I said.
B: What did you say?
A: I said you tend to complicate things – but I'm sorry I said that.
B: Oh no, I'm sorry for putting you in a position where you felt the need to . . .
A: Oh, shut up!
B: That's not very nice.
A: No, I shouldn't have said it. I'm sorry.
B: (*opens mouth but thinks better of it*) Good.

Kerin, Dorothy: founder of the Burrswood Christian Healing Centre in Sussex, this lady had one of those rare and distinctive healing ministries in which people actually got healed.

Keys of the kingdom of heaven: given by Jesus to Peter, and not, thank God, to anyone like me. I would have had to attach a huge plastic Mickey Mouse to them so that they wouldn't get lost. I know I would still have lost them, though, and everyone would have got mad at me because they were having to hang around outside the gates of heaven waiting to get in, and an angel would have had to go and wake God up to get a spare key, and he would have been mad at me as well, and then I'd have found the original ones in my other jacket and I would have been standing there going all red and defensive and the whole thing would have got most unpleasant. If you want to know why God chose one particular point in history for Jesus to come, that's probably the answer – Peter may have been somewhat impulsive and a tad Satanish at times, but he was probably very good with keys.

Kidding ourselves: what we are doing when we say such things as: 'Just in confidence and for prayer, but have you heard about Julie?'

Kidron: (1) valley which separates Jerusalem and the temple from the Mount of Olives (2) something that, three decades ago, you would have been very unwise to do in East London, according to those who knew the Kray twins.

Killing three birds with one stone: early, rejected plan to destroy Saddam Hussein by dropping the Cheeky Girls and Mick Jagger from an aircraft directly on to the top of his head. Three birds if you include Saddam.

Kirk-sessions: (1) meetings of Scottish church elders (2) *Star Trek* conferences.

Kiss: often written as 'x', which can also signify that a calculation has gone astray. Means both in some cases, never more sadly so than in the case of Judas.

Kites: might usefully be employed as the basis for a logo in some sections of the modem church as they involve lifting your arms up, being blown all over the place, getting out of control and ending up in a tangle. Alternatively, they never quite get off the ground.

Kittiwakes: birds that mate for life and make very attentive, caring parents. Might have made more sense for God to enter the world as a kittiwake rather than as a human being.

Kleptomaniacs: those most likely to benefit from the notion (if true) that God helps those who help themselves. One assumes that people suffering from this disorder will seek medical assistance and soon be taking things for it.

Knowledge, word of: spiritual gift that enables one Christian to pass divine communications to another. For those who have never heard of it, this gift is produced by God, not by Waddington's.

LEOPARD

L

Laban: banal confusion in Jacob's life whilst in exile.

Lampstands: symbols for the seven churches mentioned in the second and third chapters of the book of Revelation. There was a threat, to the church at Ephesus in particular, that these might be removed if disobedience continued in the Christian community. Similar principles might be usefully adopted in other areas of modern life. Restaurants, for instance, could be awarded up to seven 'Lampstands' for excellence in food preparation, and then receive the following official notice if the quality of their service falls below an acceptable level:

'You have a name for using fresh produce in your meals. Beware, I shall come to you with a trading standards officer and remove your lampstands from their place in the front window of your establishment.'

Land of Nod: (1) place to the east of Eden where Cain was doomed to wander after killing his brother (2) name given to the chamber where members of the cabinet met in Margaret Thatcher's time.

Lapse: spiritual decline or backsliding. Exemplified by married Christian men who, in their degenerate state, can be heard calling out to single girls in the pub, 'Come and sit on our lapse.'

Last trump: (1) sound that will wake the dead on Judgement Day (2) end of a game of cards – and everything else as well, I suppose.

Lay worker: (1) unordained, non-clerical person engaged in church-related tasks (2) chicken farmer.

Lazarus: (1) brother of Mary and Martha raised from the dead by Jesus (2) unwise choice as a name for dim-witted racehorses because when you stand by the finishing line and shout at them they have a tendency to misunderstand and come fourth.

Least in the kingdom: nominated by God using completely different criteria from that employed by most human beings, whatever the pompous git called Adrian at the top of the stepladder in this sketch might think as he addresses Phil, the humble Anglican vicar down at ground level.

P: Er, excuse me.
A: Bill, my old mate!
P: It's Phil your old mate.
A: Phil, my old mate! You all right down there?
P: Well, actually, I've just been thinking about the fact that you're famous and in demand up there at the top of the ladder, and I'm unknown and not at all in demand all the way down here on the floor. It seems very unfair.
A: You're right. It *is* unfair. And thank you so much for your concern, but I can live with it.
P: No, no, I didn't mean . . .
A: In fact, I was thinking just a minute ago that when other people look at you they probably see a miserable, worm-like runt of a no-hope clergyman –
P: Thank you very much.
A: Whereas, actually, there's so much to admire about people like you who are at the cutting edge of ministry, out there in the world where the need is greatest; your reward the joy of knowing that you're able to serve. And that is all the reward that you people with a servant heart want, isn't it?
P: Er, well, I suppose so. Actually, I could do with *some* money, and the odd scrap of recognition. You know – things like that.
A: Oooh! (*draws air in through pursed lips*) Oh, no-no-no-no-no-no-no-no! You only *think* you want those things, Bill.
P: Phil.
A: You only think you want those things, Phil. What you really want is to store up treasure in heaven, isn't it?

P: Wouldn't mind a bit down here. It's all right for you. You're up there at the top of the ladder. I'm all the way down here.
A: (*sighing*) How true that is, Bill.
P: Phil.
A: Phil. How true that is. Yes, for the foreseeable future I'm afraid I'm stuck with being an internationally known writer and speaker earning lots and lots of money and being famous and in demand all over the Christian world. (*Bravely*) And that's just something I'm going to have to live with. You know, Bill –
P: Phil.
A: I can't begin to tell you, Phil, how much I wish that I was like you. I long to have had the chance to be an obscure little nobody of a vicar making minimal impact on some seedy back-street parish in a dreary London suburb that nobody's ever heard of. Now that is a joy and a privilege, and one that I will almost certainly never be allowed to share.
P: Oh, really. All right, how about you and I swapping for a while, then? Give you a chance to enjoy my privileges for a month or two. I'll have some of your money.
A: (*earnestly*) I'd like to! I would *like* to do that!
P: Well, why don't you, then?
A: *Because I care!* Look, if I were to give in to the temptation to come down there and let you come up here, I would be exposing you to all the problems and dangers of being at the top of the ladder, and I wouldn't want to do that to you. It may seem to you, Phil –

P: You called me Phil!
A: Sorry. Bill. It may seem to you, Bill, that being one of the greatest is something you'd enjoy. What you've got to bear in mind, old chap, is that according to Scripture the one among us who thinks he's the greatest is actually the least, until such time as he realises that he's the least, at which point, of course, he becomes the greatest – unless he latches on to what has happened, in which case he becomes the least once more, thereby qualifying to be the greatest, thus starting the whole thing off all over again. Now, you don't want to get involved in all that, do you?
P: I dunno. I might if I knew what you were talking about. Anyway, the thing is –
A: So, in other words, what I'm saying is, if you really want to be the first in line, old man, the top guy, the best thing you can do is stay exactly where you are and say to yourself, 'I am a grotty, pathetic, wizened little loser. Hallelujah! My contribution to the work of God is virtually nil. Praise God! I am a smear of green scum on the rancid pool of human life. *Thank you*, Lord that I am not like him up there!' Get my drift, Bill?
P: Yes, and you could say, 'I am a big-headed pompous git and I hope I get pushed off my ladder and break my neck.'
A: (*mildly*) No need to be rude now, Bill.
P: Doh! (*walks off in disgust*)
A: (*shaking his head*) Dear, dear, spirit of resentment there, I'd say . . .

Left behind: (1) what some of us will be after the so-called rapture has happened (2) intimately close neighbour to the right behind, and a reminder to Christian children that when their bottoms are smacked unfairly by parents they should turn the other cheek.

Lent: forty-day period from Ash Wednesday to Holy Saturday, in memory of Christ's fasting in the wilderness. During this period people like to give things up. Smokers, for instance, stop smoking cigarettes and take up being irritable instead.

Lent book: one that you will never see again.

Leopard: animal well known in Israel in Bible times, mentioned by Isaiah and Jeremiah. Some of these creatures spend hours in front of the bathroom mirror every morning with lotions and skin creams. The majority realise they can't change their spots and wouldn't want to, because that's how any self-respecting leopard manages to creep up on its kill unseen.

Leotard: half-witted leopard that is almost extinct due to its habit of pirouetting up to a potential kill dressed in ballet clothes.

Let me give you a word from the Lord: (1) the Holy Spirit has given me a specific warning or encouragement or Scripture to pass on to you (2) I'm pretty sure I know exactly what you should do, and I shall enjoy exercising power over your life by dressing up my personal opinion as a message from God.

Levi: third son of Jacob and Leah, whose descendants were chosen to serve God in the tent of worship and later in the temple. It is not generally known that the Levites played a traditional 'knock-knock' game as they greeted one another at the entrance to the tent or temple. The ritual proceeded as follows:

'Knock, knock!'
'Who's there?'
'Levi.'
'Levi who?'
'Leave? I've only just got here.'

Leviathan: (1) whale or sea-monster mentioned in the book of Job (2) long-distance race for Old Testament men wearing jeans.

Liberal theologians: people who present a broad view of the narrow way, rather as estate agents use wide-angle photographs to make tiny rooms seem large.

Life: (1) life? Don't talk to me about life! (2) oh, very well, I will then. Life is complicated, simple, wonderful, dreadful, rich and poor. Whatever one believes or wants to believe, it can still be difficult to face the future when age is progressing at such a frightening speed. A little while ago my daughter asked me to put these feelings into a poem. This was the result:

The moon
The stars
Hung high in heaven for my delight
Mysterious gifts
A mobile that will draw my hands

My eyes, my life
Will teach me shape and fill my heart with wonder and with smiling

I watch
Frightened
Helpless
But secretly willing
As my foot rises, moving forward with my weight
And I realise
That at last
I am going to walk

There is not space
In this round world
To fling my hands
My heart my body
They are rockets
I will fire them to the edges of the universe and pursue the flying planets
Through the dazzling cosmos of my spirit

One road only now
It must not be the one that I have travelled
I try, I tried, but walls rise up
And strong, unyielding voices tell me
Onward is the way, you may not stand
The broad and narrow paths, all choice has vanished with the days
One road only now
I sometimes fear what I may find

Always in the past
Autumn was the richest time

But now I stumble in the fallen leaves
My body and my heart are frail
I have mislaid the magic
And imagination's power
Warm confidence that winter's coldest, darkest hour
Contains within its heart the hidden fire of spring.

Light of the world: (1) Jesus (2) painting by Holman Hunt illustrating a passage from the book of Revelation. It was recently discovered that, after completing the painting and having it hung, Hunt exclaimed, 'Oh, blast! I never got round to painting that door handle I kept meaning to put in. Now the picture's ruined!'

Limbo: place where it is claimed that unbaptized infants and those who died before the coming of Jesus practise bending backwards to pass under a horizontal bar while they wait to see what on earth is going to happen next.

Lip service: fills the devil's coffers nicely, thank you very much.

Litany: (1) series of petitions for church services or processions, usually recited by clergy and responded to by the people (2) frequent question to one who has just given up smoking.

Liturgy: (1) public worship in accordance with a prescribed form (2) not, as some non-ceremonialists have vaguely supposed, an Indian vegetable dish that might go nicely with Chicken Tikka Masala.

Livestock: (1) measure of wealth throughout the Old Testament (2) and they tick, towards their end.

Living by faith: a good idea as long as my living by faith doesn't have to be financed by someone else working twice as hard to make sure that God provides for my needs as well as theirs.

Lordship: God's cool.

Love: concept that is talked about a lot in church circles but that actually crops up in only two places in the Bible, the Old Testament and the New Testament.

Love your neighbour as yourself: whatever the height of his leylandii.

Lot: Old Testament character who lost a wife, gained a lifetime's supply of salt, set up a condiment retail business and after that – well, he never looked back.

Lucifer: highly inflammable, but no match for Jesus.

M

Macbannai: (1) son of Sheva mentioned in the second chapter of the first book of Chronicles (2) the first Jewish Scotsman on record.

Magog: (1) Satan's follower, destroyed by God in Revelation (2) devoted wife of Pagog and loving mother to all the little gogs.

Mansions: places prepared for us in heaven by Jesus. Hopefully we will not be plagued by saved or angelic estate agents from firms with names like Harp and Cloud in the Golden High Street telling us that these divine properties show great potential but might require just a little sympathetic refurbishment.

Marinated in prayer: hideous expression that arose in the eighties, and, thankfully, seems to have disappeared in recent years. One can only assume that once people had been marinated in prayer they were ready to serve.

Mariolatry: (1) idolatrous worship of the Virgin Mary (2) idolatrous worship of Nintendo games.

Mary: heroic mother of Jesus. Luke tells us that, on being told by the angel that she was greatly blessed, Mary was immediately deeply troubled, thus setting a pattern for the lives of most Christians ever since.

Mary on a donkey: virgin on the ridiculous.

Mass: (1) a celebration of the Eucharist, especially in the Roman Catholic Church (2) E over C squared, according to Einstein.

Maybe we can find some grass: (1) what Obad said to Obadiah in 1 Kings 18:5 when they needed to keep the mules and horses alive (2) frequent item of dialogue between hippies in the sixties when they went out on a Friday night.

Medad: (1) one of the men on whom the Spirit descended after Moses had complained about shortage of food in the eleventh chapter of Numbers (2) the person who is married to Memum.

Meetings: see **Methodism**.

Mere Christianity: (1) book on the basics of Christian belief by Clive Staples Lewis, literary scholar, novelist and popular theologian (2) book about the very special problems faced by believers who feel led to live beside lakes.

Methodism: see **Meetings**.

Microphone: (1) technical item of voice-enhancing equipment that Jesus never had the benefit of using. (2) useful for those who are leading meetings when they need to use a soupy, buzzy, thrilling voice to ask people in the assembly to perform such activities as turning to the person next to them and exchanging clothes.

Militant Christianity: rather worrying sometimes, especially when it gives certain individuals the opportunity to express their violent tendencies in the context of loving outreach to the secular world. The following popular hymn, slightly reconstructed, expresses this point:

> Every Christian soldier
> Needs to know for sure
> Unlike George Bush Junior
> Why we went to war
> Time to face reality
> Time to face the facts
> We will never save the lost
> By bombing them with tracts
> All we Christian soldiers
> Need to know for sure
> Unlike George and Tony
> Why we went to war.

Miracle: (1) extraordinary event attributed to some supernatural agency. Jesus performed and performs many miracles (2) frequent airline users who have had problems with the non-arrival of baggage will not be surprised to hear that 'miracle' is an anagram of 'reclaim.'

Mission Impossible: (1) television series popular in the sixties and seventies about a team of professionals who undertook apparently impossible undercover missions for the government (2) a fair description, on the face of it, for the task that Jesus was presented with by his father:

GOD: I have a mission for you.
JESUS: Okay, fire away.
GOD: Your mission, if you care to accept it, is to go into the world and preach for three years.
JESUS: Doesn't sound too tricky.
GOD: Well, as a result of what you do down there I want the world changed. Eventually I'd like to see at least one Christian church in practically every village and town in the western world, and a fair proportion of the east as well. Within two thousand years there must be millions and millions of people following your teaching and living by your inspiration and spiritual presence in their lives.
JESUS: Er, right. Three years, you said?
GOD: That's right.
JESUS: Okay, so presumably you'll put me in an age where transport and communication technology has reached its peak, so that I'll be able to –
GOD: Well, no. Actually, it'll be first century Palestine. Mostly on foot. The occasional mule. And you'll have

a team of twelve. Fishermen, tax collectors, that sort of thing.

JESUS: Fishermen and tax collectors?

GOD: That sort of thing.

JESUS: I see. And between us we're going to change the world.

GOD: Turn it upside down, yes.

JESUS: And, just as a matter of interest, what happens at the end of my three years of preaching?

GOD: Ah, now we come to the really difficult bit of the job.

JESUS: There's a *more* difficult bit of the job? And what might that be?

GOD: Well, first of all, are you willing to go?

JESUS: Of course, if that's what you want.

GOD: Good! Right. I'm very pleased. Now, I'm afraid this is what has to happen . . .

Misused prayer: prayer used for any purpose other than communicating with God, three fairly common examples being gossip, avoidance of a real but uncomfortable issue and preaching. The husband and wife in the dialogue that follows are setting out to publicly perform a positive sketch about Christian marriage, but find themselves ambushed by their own problems as a couple. In this case prayer is apparently being used as a not very subtle disguise for conflict:

HUSBAND: (*to audience*) Ladies and gentlemen, the sketch we are about to perform for you is one that combats the negative view so prevalent nowadays of marriage in general and Christian

marriage in particular. (*to wife*) Right, off you go.
WIFE: (*after a pause*) What do you mean – off *I* go? You're the one who starts.
H: (*scans script*) No, that was ages ago. We've changed it since then. I can't believe you don't remember. We went through it over and over again, and each time we did it –
W: You started.
H: I did not!
W: I'm sorry, but you did.
H: You can be as sorry as you like. You can be awash with penitence, but I didn't start it, and I'm not going to say I did just to keep the peace.
W: I would think that very noble of you, darling, if I wasn't aware that your memory tends to be somewhat selective. *You* are the one who starts.
H: I am not.
W: You are.
H: I'm not.
W: I'm sorry, but you are.
H: Why do you always apologise when you think you're right?
W: Why do you always hiss through your teeth when you know you're wrong?
H: (*hisses exasperatedly through his teeth*) I do *not* always – look, don't you think this is a bit unseemly in front of all these people?
W: Yes, I absolutely agree, and I would be very interested to know what you, as the one who is totally in the wrong, suggest that we do about it.
H: (*somewhat grimly*) Well, this is a Christian meeting; I think we ought to resolve our differences through prayer.

W: (*equally grim*) I agree. Go on, then – you start.
H: No, you should start, because it's – oh, let's not go through all that again. I'll start. (*addresses audience*) Please excuse us for a moment or two while we just pray through to victory. (*Both take up praying stances etc. Husband makes all the smiley, sippy noises that precede prayer in certain circles*) Mmm, right, okay . . . Lord, we just want to thank you for my wife, and all the great qualities that she so modestly conceals. We ask now that she should have a right view in this matter of who starts. May a real healing of memories take place. And may she find a new and deeper understanding of that wonderful passage in Ephesians where wives are commanded to submit to their husbands. Amen! Now, let's get going and –
W: (*interrupting*) Lord, we want to rebuke all stubbornness, arrogance and chauvinistically deliberate misinterpretation of Scripture at this time. We bring to mind those many occasions when certain of us have gone on and on about being right about something and then found that we were wrong all the time. And we particularly recall, in a moment of silence, that occasion when one of us insisted that he could undertake very complicated work that should have been done by a professional plumber, and as a result ruined a week of decorating that had just been finished by the other one of us. Vouchsafe us not a repetition of that sort of nonsense, we beseech thee, oh Lord. Amen.
H: Oh, that's a good one, Lord, that is! May your Holy Spirit just remind us who it is that becomes

a world expert on unnecessary expense as far as yours truly thine humble servant speaking at the moment is concerned, and then when the holiday comes, blows a great chunk of thy bounty on summer frocks, despite what the head of the woman has to say about it. Mayhap, Lord, some of us have forgotten our marriage vows, and especially that little word 'obey.'

W: Or perhaps, Lord, others of us have forgotten that slightly longer word 'cherish.' Some of us could do with a bit of cherishing, Lord, instead of constant criticism, chronic meanness, and *stupid* –

H: Forgive us when we are abusive.

W: And when we are sanctimoniously self-righteous, Lord.

H: Thank you for your command that we should not judge others, lest we ourselves be judged.

W: (*after a little inner wrestling*) Oh, we might as well let him have his own way, Lord. He'll only go into mega-sulk overdrive and start doing those pathetic shuddering sighs all over the place, and I couldn't stand that. Amen!

H: (*very pleased*) Amen! I'm glad you've seen sense, and you realise now that it's me who starts.

W: What! But you said – oh, never mind. You start.

H: (*ruefully*) Perhaps we won't bother with the positive marriage sketch . . .

Moabite: (1) one of the inhabitants of Moab, the land defeated by King David, as recorded in 2 Samuel 8 (2) a nasty peck from an extinct flightless bird that was once native to New Zealand.

Monogamy: (1) the God-approved practice or state of being married to one person at a time (2) replaced in some modern communities by 'stereogamy', which allows you to hear your spouse speaking to you from both sides at the same time.

Mooing: strange, sonorous, moaning sound used by some Christians in extempore prayer groups to signal their assent to the content and direction of a particular petition.

Morning Star: (1) name for Jesus used by Isaiah and Peter, and by Jesus speaking of himself in the twentieth chapter of Revelation (2) Eamonn Holmes.

Moses: great Old Testament leader of the Israelites, who climbed Mount Nebo in order to glimpse the promised land, then turned to sing a couple of verses of his farewell song: 'I did it Yahweh!'

Mother Carey's chickens: general term for nervous Anglicans before Rowan Williams took over.

Mother Theresa: anagram of 'Heart rest home.'

Mothering Sunday: (1) originally a day on which Christians returned to their church of origin (2) the one day in the year when hardworking mothers are prevented from enjoying a relaxing day at the end of the week because they are woken up by excited small children at five o'clock in the morning and expected to be excitedly grateful for warm orange juice, cold tea, and other strange combinations of breakfast items on a tray with no lip that usually ends up tipping messy things on to the bed.

Moving in . . . : strange evangelical phrase which appears to mean 'spiritually engaged in.' Thus: 'I am moving in healing/discernment/molasses/prophetic basketball/circles.'

Mushroom: of some interest to Christians two or three decades ago, when it was suggested by a tabloid newspaper that God might be a mushroom. This confusion presumably arose because mushrooms appear suddenly where they have not appeared before, and you have to make sure you've got a real one because the others are likely to be very bad for you.

Mustering at Micmash: (1) what the Philistines were doing when Saul disobeyed the Lord by making a burnt offering, as described in the thirteenth chapter of the first book of Samuel (2) getting together to eat an Irish vegetable dish.

My Bible says . . . : oddly possessive prelude to disagreeing with someone else's interpretation of Scripture.

My Faith: (1) what I believe without seeing, an essential aspect of Christian living (2) what Chris Eubank replies when asked what he sees in his shaving mirror each morning.

Myths: (1) traditional narratives usually involving supernatural or imaginary persons and embodying popular ideas on natural or social phenomena. Paul advised both Timothy and Titus to have nothing to do with such things (2) female moths.

NATIVITY SCENE

N

Naaman: proud Syrian general with leprosy, who insisted on choosing his own swimming style, but, after taking advice from his little maid, was very relieved that he had agreed to settle for the crawl.

Name above all names: (1) Jesus Christ (2) aardvark.

Name it and claim it: and do your best to blame it when it doesn't work, more often than not.

Nation: word that, for some reason, is almost invariably used in formal Christian situations instead of the word 'country', presumably because 'nation' has a more monumental and significant ring to it.

Nativity scenes: presentations which, in the case of infants, commonly involve such distractions as shepherds throwing up in public, wise men forgetting their lines, and the baby Jesus having to be recast as a wandering star because he keeps getting out of the manger for a little explore around.

Near death experience: (1) journeys up long tunnels to meet shining beings and such like, who then offer choices about whether to come back or stay or whatever (2) life.

Nebuchadnezzar: king of Babylon. Went through a seven year period of living like an animal, during which his hair and nails grew to unmanageable lengths and he spent most of each day consuming grass. Acknowledged nowadays as a forerunner of the hippie movement.

Nelson: nineteenth century admiral of the British fleet who, bearing in mind his relationship with Lady Hamilton, and judging from his statue in Trafalgar Square, seems to have arrived at a very literal interpretation of Jesus' advice concerning temptation to adultery in the fifth chapter of Matthew's gospel.

Never Never Land: world whose inhabitants have no wish to grow up, and have decided to turn their backs on the real world (See also **Synods in England and Scotland**).

New age: (1) tag attached to all sorts of dodgy modern practices, usually connected with the occult. Lip-lickingly popular with a good proportion of those who disapprove of such things (2) what we all are every birthday.

New curates: those who may be unfortunate enough to find themselves replacing a truly wonderful man or woman, the like of whom is unlikely to be seen ever again in the world or the universe, let alone this parish.

New dispensation: (1) period since the death and ascension of Jesus, during which grace abounds (2) a fresh packet of corn-plasters and some more of that cream that clears the old trouble up in no time.

New Frontiers: (1) a network of non-denominational churches (2) replacement plastic surgery performed on an alien.

New Year: a time when one might take back an unwanted present to be exchanged. For those who have newly understood the meaning of Christmas it might be a time for taking an unwanted present and an unwanted past to God and asking him to exchange it for a much more desirable future.

Nice: generally regarded as faint, rather anaemic praise, but Christians would do well to appreciate that, in addition to being awesome and mighty and omniscient and omnipotent and all-seeing and triumphant and impossible to look on, God really is extremely kind and nice.

Nicodemus: nervous Jewish Irishman encountered by Jesus in the middle of the night (See also **Born again Christian**).

A B C D E F G H I J K L M N O P Q R S T U V W X Y Z

Nightingale: included here because on several occasions recently I have been drawn from the bosom of sleep at around two o'clock in the morning by an unbelievably mellifluous sound emanating from somewhere in the hedge of tall trees outside my bedroom window. This extravagant, rippling melody is like the outpouring of a heart so abundantly filled with joy that it has no choice but to overflow, and it is actually the song of a nightingale.

At least, I think it's a nightingale.

Well, I suppose I'm about eighty-five percent sure that it must be a nightingale. All right, I have to confess that I cannot be absolutely confident about the identity of this bird, but the thing is, it makes a beautiful sound in the very early hours of the morning. It sings at night, and it would probably continue to do so if there was a gale. What else can I say?

Okay, I suppose there is an outside chance that what I could be dealing with here is an insomniac blackbird. The song of a blackbird is said to be similar to that of a nightingale. It seems unlikely, though, don't you think? Are blackbirds known for their inability to sleep? And even if they are, they wouldn't end up singing their hearts out with joy in the middle of the night, would they? You don't do that when you can't sleep for being depressed. It must be a nightingale. It must be.

But how can I be absolutely sure? It's far too dark at that time of night to see a little brown bird in a thick hedge. Short of persuading an

A B C D E F G H I J K L M N O P Q R S T U V W X Y Z

unwilling expert on the songs of British birds to hang around in my bedroom on the off-chance of a performance on that particular night, or spending a load of money to hire some of that infra-red equipment for seeing things in the dark, or recording the sound the creature makes to play back to the expert who wasn't particularly keen on spending the night in my bedroom, I don't see how I can ever be truly certain that what I am hearing is a nightingale.

I bet John Keats never had this problem – well, I say that. Maybe he did. Maybe he buttonholed a friend one morning and put the problem squarely to him.

'The thing is, Eric, there's this bird that sings outside my bedroom window every night. I think it's a nightingale, and I'm really keen to write a moving but fairly miserable ode on it. But only if I can be sure that it's definitely not something else. What I really don't want is to make a plonker of myself by going on and on about a light-winged Dryad of the trees singing of summer in full-throated ease if it turns out to have been a different bird altogether. *Ode to a jetlagged starling doing nightingale impressions* doesn't have quite the same ring to it. Do you get my drift?'

No doubt Eric, being a sensible sort of fellow, would have said something along the lines of: 'John, my old mate, what does it matter if you can't be absolutely sure? You hear a beautiful song in the middle of the night. It's probably a nightingale. You want to write about it. Get on with it. Have a quick beaker full of the warm South to get you in the mood, and then put quill to paper. You'll be done in no time. Sorted or what!'

Eric's point is a good one. Why does it matter to me that I am unable to conclusively identify the source of such beauty? Why can I not relax and surrender myself to the enjoyment of an experience that needs no labels? A rose is a rose is a rose, whatever you decide to call it. That's more or less what Shakespeare said, and he was right. I need to battle with this completion neurosis of mine.

A very old friend died a while ago. Before I became a follower of Jesus he filled a parenting gap in my life so effectively that my self-esteem was able to find a tiny platform from which to face and tackle a world that appeared very threatening. Later, when I became a Christian, I went through a compartmentalising phase common to many new converts in the sixties. Anything or anyone that could not be given a narrowly evangelical label had no real place in what I short-sightedly thought of as the spiritual world. My friend, not being a Christian, was one of those who must necessarily be excluded from this world until such time as he saw the light and asked Jesus into his heart. God forgive my ignorance and my stupid pomposity. I was given my friend at a time when I needed him most, and his love and support came from the heart of God. He offered me much more than a cup of water and he will be rewarded accordingly.

The song of a nightingale and the love of God, beautiful things that simply fill our hearts. It doesn't matter which direction they come from and labels don't change in the slightest.

Nike: son of the great prophet, Adidas. Best known and most useful quote is from chapter one, verse one of the book of Nike: 'Just do it!'

Noah: (1) Old Testament character who, with his family and representative couples of every species of animal, was allowed to escape the flood that God sent to destroy all the evil people in the world (2) what Gazza says when he disagrees.

Non-conformist churches: denominations that have broken away from spiritually atrophied mainline churches in order to be allowed to atrophy in a manner that is in accordance with their own understanding of Scripture.

Non-conformist ministers: rare, in any denomination.

Norman: what the font at the back of our church is, as opposed to the vicar, who is Frank.

Nothing, nothing, absolutely nothing, nothing is too difficult for Thee!: line of a Christian song which is absolutely true, leaving aside, of course, any question of me having anything to do with my cousin after what he said to me in the late fifties – or was it the early sixties?

Notices: essential practical details shared from the front during a church service. A phenomenon seen at its fascinating best in those churches where the minister is likely to be corrected on every point from the body of the church by various members of the congregation.

Nursery Rhymes: children's chants that can occasionally be adapted for church use, as in:

> The Reverend Jack Horner ate plums in a corner
> And said, 'I'll be dead controversial
> At Christmas this year, I shall preach on my fear
> That it's all getting far too commercial!'

OPEN TO THE SPIRIT

[see also HEAVENLY HOST]

Obadiah:
'Knock, knock!'
'Who's there?'
'A professional Yes-man seeking employment.'
'Well, what's your name?'
'Obadiah.'
'If I'm going to employ you I need to know your full name!'
'Gree.'
'Obadiah Gree? That's a ridiculous name.'
'Obadiah Gree.'

Obedience: (1) curious item of fossilised spiritual behaviour, still practised by the odd individual Christian, and by fanatical members of one or two of the more obscure sects (2) a difficult but essential aspect of following Jesus. For instance, I remember being in a northern branch of WH Smith, that well known chain of shops that has been selling newspapers, books and stationery for years. That night I was due to be speaking at a church in the town, but having arrived rather earlier than expected I had decided to look for a book to read on the train during my return journey on the following day.

The books in this shop were arranged in freestanding racks so that you could walk all the way round each one. Every rack had a label in a frame attached to the top of the unit, informing customers about the type of books it contained. Apart from the largest section of all, which was General Fiction, it seemed that Diet, Fitness, Holidays, House-purchasing and Antique-collecting had taken over the world as far as the book market was concerned. I discovered that there was one very small section allocated to Religion, and Christianity occupied an even smaller space within that category, sandwiched alphabetically between Buddhism and Fortune-telling. The books in the Christian bit were a dull, colourless, embarrassed clutch of volumes. They huddled miserably together like mouldy potatoes being sold by mistake in a sweetshop, all too conscious, perhaps, that drab worthiness has scant appeal in today's commercial world.

As a little parable, I reflected, it speaks volumes.

Groaning at my unintentional pun I moved on towards the Fiction section, steadfastly avoiding a strong temptation to drift sideways into the stationery department. Why? Okay, I might as well confess. I am a stationery junkie. I love it all. I am close to salivating even as I type these words and find myself fantasising wildly. I would have bought ridiculous quantities of rubber bands, drawing pins, sticky labels, paperclips, erasers, self-adhesive envelopes and pencil-sharpeners if I had not been so heavily sedated by the usual morning dose of my wife's common sense. There should be groups for people like me.

Fortunately, browsing through racks of books is equally absorbing as far as I am concerned, and I was soon lost to the real world as I began to explore a very smart new paper-backed edition of novels and short stories by P.G. Wodehouse. He is a sublime exponent of English as the written word, and my favourite comic writer if one excludes Jerome K. Jerome, who was the author of that one supreme comedy classic *Three Men in a Boat*.

Because books are invariably organised alphabetically in shops of this kind, the works of Wodehouse are usually to be found on the far right hand side of the very bottom shelf of the fiction section. Such was the case here in WH Smith, and it was as I rose from my genuflecting perusal of the master's books at this lower level that I became aware of a woman standing on the other side of the rack. She had her back to me and her head was buried in a book, but there was something very familiar about the cut of the short honey-coloured hair, the shape and slope of the shoulders and the square-shouldered, navy style jacket with piping on the shoulders. I moved a little further along my side of the rack in order to get a better view. Now I could see the woman clearly. Yes. I was right. I did recognise her, and suddenly all I could think of was how I was going to escape from this shop without her seeing me.

This lady (I shall call her Irene) was a Christian who had once lived in the same part of the world as me. She was also one of the most annoying people I had ever met. She had a high, penetrating voice, like a fighter plane diving out of control, and some kind of profound conversational disability that prevented her from allowing anyone else to finish what they were saying. On first encountering her a few years ago I had attempted to embark on a number of sentences, but found each one scythed effortlessly to the ground by that razor-sharp blade of a voice. I have always enjoyed hearing what other people have to say, but I was certainly not used to the treatment I got from Irene at that first meeting. Each one of these clinical interruptions was like a physical blow to the head, or, more honestly, to the ego. In the end I gave up and spent the rest of the conversation grunting, nodding, shaking my head, seething inwardly and marvelling at the extraordinary degree of self-absorption that must lie behind such total disregard for what another person has to say. I had no idea what she thought of me, although when we met at church functions she always seemed to be pleased to see me, and was guaranteed to present a number of loud opinions for my grunting, nodding, head-shaking, inwardly seething attention.

I asked myself what on earth she could be doing here in this town, today of all days. Looking warily at her now over the top of the rack, I realised for the first time just how much I disliked the woman. The very thought of contact with her set my nerves jangling. Never mind, if I was quick and careful I could slip away before she took her head out of that book and started to squeak delightedly about us meeting up here of all places.

My route was clear. Down past Diets I went, turned right at Holidays, hurried along the aisle between Antiques and Biographies, across the littered no man's land of newspapers and magazines, past the tills and the counters until suddenly I was in the blessed open air and heading for a place where I could get coffee, safe from the possibility of having to endure Irene and her terrible voice. Thank goodness for that! I didn't get as far as the coffee place.

'You are not your own.'

What does that mean?

'You don't like talking to Irene because her voice and her manner annoy you, but you are not in the business of only spending time with people who make you feel good. Not if you ever meant it when you said that you had some serious idea about following me. Suppose I want you to be available to talk to Irene? Will you go back into the shop and make that possible?'

What – now?

'Now.'

Before having coffee?

'Before having coffee.'

But Irene is so – so . . .

'How significant is the Christian section in the presentation of your own life? Is it a small, sad little category tucked between Buddhism and Fortune-telling that no one else really notices because it takes up so little space? Because if it is . . .'

Oh, all right!

Muttering darkly about whether I was dealing with the Holy Spirit or my imagination, I turned on my heel and went back to WH Smith. Irene was still there, standing beside a different subject-rack, deeply engrossed in yet another book. I could not quite bring myself to go up to her and initiate a conversation, but I followed her at a short distance as she wandered distractedly from rack to rack, placing myself in positions where she could not fail to see me if she looked up from her reading. But I seemed to have become invisible. At one point she appeared to look straight through my body (no easy task) as though it were transparent. Finally she left the store and I breathed a sigh of relief. I had been available, I had not been arrested for stalking and I had not had to spend half an hour listening to Irene's out-of-control Spitfire impression.

So what had it all been about? If, as I suspect, it was a test of obedience and availability, then I scored about five and a half out of ten.

As I left the shop and headed for my delayed coffee, I found that I was haunted by one unexpected and uncomfortable question. Could it be that *she* had been avoiding *me*?

Oblivion: nothing to worry about.

Oh, my lover is radiant and ruddy: statement from the fifth chapter of the Song of Solomon, presumably spoken by the great king after finding that his girlfriend had fallen asleep in front of the gas fire.

Okay, so you think, just because there's no evidence of divine intervention in your life, and none of your prayers are being answered, and everything's gone wrong, and your spiritual state is moribund, and you feel completely alone in the universe, that God is nowhere to be found, whereas actually you will find that he is vibrantly, clearly, unmistakably, visibly present before your very eyes at this precise moment in full Technicolor if you just work through the seventeen easy to follow steps outlined in this book: slightly exaggerated example of a type of book title that we are seeing quite a lot of at present. No problem, of course, about letting people know that God is closer than they might think, but perhaps we should beware of rationalising silences and gaps that are there for a reason. Before Gideon was called, for instance, the voice of the Lord had not been heard in Israel for many years.

Old Nick: (1) the devil (2) ex-presenter of *They Think It's All Over* (3) Victorian police station.

Old Testament: the part of the Christian Bible containing the Scriptures of the Hebrews. Must, of course, be regarded as inerrant, infallible and a guide to daily living. That is why modern churches regularly take their disobedient teenagers out and stone them; bears are trained to attack kids who are cheeky to bald preachers; whole villages of unbelievers, men, women and children, are put to the sword and followers of Jesus never eat pork.

Open to the Spirit: (1) familiar with twenty or more songs from Mission Praise (2) tentatively willing to consider the possibility of a short and carefully controlled time of informal prayer and worship at a point where there will be no real damage done to the fabric of the service.

Opportunities: what we are urged to make the most of in the fourth chapter of Colossians. Can be a little overdone by some. There are those, for instance, who invite non-Christians round for a meal and use it as an 'opportunity.' Their guests hear *Bringing in the sheaves* played on the doorbell, they wipe their feet on a doormat that says 'Welcome to the kingdom of God', they have the gospel preached to them violently and at length via the grace and they drink from coffee mugs

A B C D E F G H I J K L M N O P Q R S T U V W X Y Z

covered in John 3:16. Finally, after the washing-up has been done, their hosts wipe the kitchen surfaces down and say coyly to their guests, 'Would you believe me if I told you that your sins could be wiped away as quickly and easily as I just wiped away those little smears of tomato sauce?'

Optical Illusionist: (1) a magician. If a Christian performer, might do excitingly symbolic things like cutting a bit of rope then magically joining it together in order to subtly illustrate that we are cut off from God until we become Christians, at which point we are joined to him again (2) some believers disapprove of secular magicians because they deliberately deceive, but have failed to reflect on the fact that no one could be more straightforward and honest than a man who announces that he is about to deceive you. Contrast this approach with that of some evangelists and preachers, where you are left to discover this for yourself.

Original sin: (1) that committed by Adam which brought the whole of mankind under judgement (2) something that is forbidden, but more interesting and innovative than usual.

Out of his will: (1) behaving in a way that is contrary to the express wishes of God (2) hard luck – turns out you won't be able to pay off the mortgage after all.

Outworking: (1) visible manifestation of the purpose or will of God (2) back at teatime.

Overhead projector: often referred to as an OHP Confusion with the term OAP is a bad idea, as

A B C D E F G H I J K L M N O P Q R S T U V W X Y Z

discovered by a man in one of our local churches who announced the following: 'I have been going through the OAPs in our church and it has become clear to me that many of them are simply no use to us any more. They are elderly, shabby, difficult to understand, poorly put together, old fashioned and often theologically unsound. Some of them are literally falling apart. I have weeded out a number of these redundant OAPs and I suggest that we store them in the church cupboard until the autumn. Have a look through if you wish, and feel free to take home any that you fancy, otherwise I shall dispose of them on the church bonfire.'

Ozone: (1) essential atmospheric layer that is developing holes because of the use by human beings of inappropriate gases (2) this section of the book.

A B C D E F G H I J K L M N O P Q R S T U V W X Y Z

PILLARS OF THE CHURCH

P

Pantomime: event that is completely different from a church service. In a pantomime lots of slightly nervous people sitting in rows are asked to do rather silly things, call out childish responses, join in with a number of banal songs and suspend their disbelief in characters whose manner on stage is significantly different from the way they would behave in real life. Whereas, in church . . . er . . . never mind.

Parables: stories that entertain you at the front door while the truth slips in through a side window and sandbags you from behind.

Patterns: patterns of the most profound things can be detected in the ordinary events of our lives. Here is a childhood memory that contains all the elements of the Fall.

It is 1954. I am six years old. I am on my way to the library to take my books back. To get there I have to go through the back door, past the rhododendrons at the end of the lawn, out of our front gate, along the path made from bricks, right through to the end of the High Street, and across the grassy bit of common that starts after the chemist's shop at the end of the village. I like going to the library because I love reading books. Books are chunky and rich and full of treasure.

Today, though, there is a problem. My two books are late back. The date has gone beyond the month and day stamped in red on the piece of paper stuck inside their front covers. I am a bit worried. The lady at the library got quite cross once before when I took my books back late. This time I have got a very good excuse for bringing them back late if I want to use it, but I am not sure if I am going to want to say the words that will make the excuse work.

I arrive at the library and walk up to the lady. She is sitting behind her desk at the far end of the narrow room lined with shelves that are stuffed full with all those delicious books. But it is a little bit like school, and the lady in charge is a little bit like a teacher. I hold out my books and say the words I have been practising in my head ever since I walked out of my house.

A B C D E F G H I J K L M N O P Q R S T U V W X Y Z

'I've brought my books back, but I'm afraid they're late because my Nana died and we've been too busy.'

Feelings fill me up like water rushing into a glass from a tap when you turn it on full. One is a feeling of shock because I just heard my own voice saying the terrible, terrible thing that surely cannot be true. I have said it out loud for the first time, so maybe it is true after all.

But how can Nana be dead? *How*? How can my Nana have gone away forever? How can it be true that the shining, warm, cosily all right bit of life that was being with Nana can never happen again? What point will there be in the tall green buses setting out to travel the fourteen miles from Tunbridge Wells to Heathfield if there is no one sitting on the top deck getting more and more excited about walking up Nana's drive and knocking on her front door?

There is a quiet place inside myself where I know that this awful thing is true. Mummy told me after she told my brother John. She said we all have to be very brave. I don't know what that means. Will being brave take away the feeling that I have swallowed a big, soft black cloud, a black cloud that is sitting in my stomach making me feel heavy and giddy with fear and darkness? I don't think it will. Nothing ever will.

Another feeling is a feeling of being ashamed. I could have brought my books back before the date on the inside of the cover. Secretly I know I could have. It was nothing to do with the bad thing that has happened to my Nana. But the other thing I am sure of is that a dead Nana must be one of the best ways of not getting into trouble. Who is going to tell off a little boy whose Nana has just died? I don't think even the lady at the library will. This is a naughty thing that I am doing, but I don't want to be told off.

The lady in charge of the library puts a very kind face on and tells me that I mustn't worry this time. Just choose some new books and take them home.

It is then that I have one more feeling, and it is a very strange one. Part of it is to do with finding out that very bad things really do happen. They actually do happen to people like me, and I did not know this until I heard myself say out loud that Nana was dead. I had worried sometimes that they might, but I was never quite sure, and when bad things did look as if they might happen my mummy and daddy made everything seem all right. This is going to be different. There is nothing they can ever say about Nana being dead that will make it all right.

The other part of this strange feeling is to do with hearing myself make up an excuse for bringing my books back late. Using Nana as an excuse! I do bad things. Secret things. I have just done one. Nana would not have liked it. I expect I will probably do some more bad things.

The thing that is so, so strange about this feeling is that, suddenly, right there in the middle of the library, in front of the lady in charge, I feel as if I have got no clothes on. Imagine that. No clothes! It is a sad, lost,

A B C D E F G H I J K L M N O P Q R S T U V W X Y Z

> panicky, bad-dream sort of feeling. Dark, terrible things can happen, and there is good and bad inside me. I want my Nana back, but if I saw her coming into the library now I think I would want to hide. I feel undressed and ashamed.

Pentecostals: people who may well have arrived at the denomination of their choice by a process of elimination.

Penultimate supper: quite a nice occasion, but er . . . nothing to write home about really.

Pews: largely Victorian, wooden bench seats that are gradually being replaced with chairs in many churches. Might well seem to an outsider that the term actually refers to a troublesome family that is continually being ejected from one church, only to appear in another and be thrown out all over again. As in:

'In my view our main priority has to be getting rid of the Pews. They make everyone feel uncomfortable, they take up too much space, they're ugly and dull to look at, they're hard and unyielding, they're extremely difficult to get away from when you need to go to the toilet in a hurry, it takes a crowbar to shift them from their original position and most people you ask find them a pain in the backside.'

Pillar of the church: (1) person who is consistent and reliable in their commitment to the well-being of the congregation (2) big thick thing that holds everything up and restricts vision.

A B C D E F G H I J K L M N O P Q R S T U V W X Y Z

Pillock of the church: big thick thing that holds everything up and restricts vision.

Pop groups: a modern phenomenon, including one band whose existence was prophesied in Old Testament days. God threatened to play their albums repeatedly in the hearing of those of his people who were disobedient. As Moses declared, 'The Lord will afflict you with Madness . . . '

Poverty: some are born poor, some acquire poverty, some have poverty thrust upon them, some have never experienced poverty, some had better read the twenty-fifth chapter of Matthew's gospel before it's too late.

Pray and Display: special car park designed for use by modern Pharisees.

Prayer of Humble Access: (1) magnificently worded Anglican prayer offered immediately prior to the celebration of communion (2) pathetic request from a husband and father living under the yoke of a wife and teenage daughters, that the bathroom might possibly be free for him to enter and use at some indefinable point in the future.

Prelate: (1) talk foolishly about the Spanish ecclesiastical dignitary (2) on time or early.

Prodigal Son: (1) central figure in one of the parables of Jesus. He wasted his money in riotous living and was welcomed with open arms by his father when he finally got hungry, repented and returned home (2) deeply resented by the fatted calf (3) anagram of 'no God spiral.'

Prophecy: (1) speaking out for God (2) the gift most earnestly to be desired, according to Saint Paul – sadly for those of us with material aspirations, not a Porsche or a Lear jet.

Prophetic macramé: (1) one in a long list of activities that, it is claimed by those who presumably must know, have a prophetic element. These include banner-making, fabric analysis, worshipful dance and flower arranging. Why God should choose to express himself specifically through these means is a secret that has not been shared with most of us, but we wait in humility to be enlightened (2) presumably the overwhelmingly preferred activity at that great Christian festival, String Harvest, where the chorus that is sung more than any other is:

Bind Us Together, Lord
Bind us together
With cords that cannot be broken, but can be arranged into a very pleasingly complex and surprisingly practical pattern . . .

Prosperity gospel: very popular, of course, but an evil and dangerous contradiction in terms. We in the developed countries are already rich beyond measure in comparison with those who live on the edge of starvation in third world countries. We can be the answer to their prayers for greater prosperity if we wish. Do we wish?

Pulpit: (1) raised, enclosed platform from which a preacher delivers a sermon (2) useful suggestion as to what might be done with quite a large proportion of what we loosely call Christian literature.

Putting to death the old man: (1) destroying the unredeemed person that each of us was before conversion (2) assassinating your dad.

QUEEN OF THE SOUTH

Q

Quadragesima: first Sunday in Lent. All over the country at this time of year Christians can be heard cheerily calling out from their windows, 'Happy Quadragesima, everybody!'

Queen of the South: Scottish football team likely to do well in the league according to a biblical prophecy in the gospel of Matthew: 'The queen of the South will rise . . .'

Queensland: a sun soaked state in the land of Australia where Bridget and I undertook a speaking tour with all four of our children.

Subsequently we discovered that, amazingly, there is a Scripture pertaining to this visit:

'And the Lord saith to Adrian, "Leave your country and your cushy little number, and go to the land wherein mine people shower nineteen time a day and throweth prawns on the barbie, whatever that mighteth mean."

And Adrian did winge, being a Pom, and did say, "Hold on a minute, Lord, what about all these issue what I've begatted?"

For Adrian and his wife Bridget (she who doeth most of the work) had begatted Matthew, and they had begatted Joseph, and they had begatted David, and they had accidentally begatted Katy, so that the tribe of Plass increaseth mightily.

And the Lord replieth, "Hard luck, mate! You should have thought about that before you started begatting, shouldn't you? Nevertheless, I seeth your problem, so you may bringeth 'em all with you."

Then Adrian did wax sarcastic, and did say, "Oh, yes, Lord, we've got thousands of pounds to throweth about, I don't thinketh. And even if we had, where would we pitch our tents whensoever we arriveth, or will it be like poor old Mary in Bethlehem, when she foundeth you'd blown the budget on angel effects, and couldn't affordeth bed and breakfast?"

And the Lord was much enangered by this cheek, and did humble Adrian with a plague of final demands, so that Adrian throweth himself on the Lord, who saith, "Get off!"

And Adrian saith, "Oh, God, I'll do anything to get out of this blinking country."

So the Lord saith, "Right! On the financial side I have been stirring up churches in one of the denominations in Australia (I've been meaning to do that for some time anyway) and one of mine servants there will arrangeth an little tour which should cover the costs nicely."

And Adrian got all spiritual and saith, "Shall we be wafted by thine Spirit to this far country wherein thou wisheth us to serve thee, so that in the twinkling of an eye we shall be there present?"

And the Lord replieth, "No, you can fly Qantas out and Virgin back, with a stop over at Singapore. Taketh it or leave it."

Then Adrian cried out with a loud voice in sore distress, saying, "Knoweth thou not, Lord, that last time we flew Qantas they losteth *all* mine luggage, and I did mine first talk dressed in someone else's shorts?"

But the Lord prevailed, and thus it came to pass that the tribe of Plass did journey to the land of 'Four X' and Rolf Harris songs, and they did pitch their tents in the city of Margate, which lieth beside the sea. Then Adrian became puffed up with pride even more than usual, saying, "By mine own efforts have I brought us here. Well done, me!"

And God sent a plague of mosquitoes to eat tender parts of all the Plasses, and great was the scratching and itching thereof.

Next, the Lord sent a plague of Queensland heat which beateth down on the soft white

Poms, until they resembleth human tomatoes. And they were sore – well, just sore.

And Adrian goeth into a chemist's shop, wherein a serving man saith, "Here's the stuff to stop the mozzies biting, and here's the stuff to put on after it hasn't worked. Here's the stuff to protect you from the sun, and here's the stuff to put on after you've got burned."

And behold the Plasses buyeth great hats, like unto that worn by Ritchie Richardson, captain of the West Indian team that stuffeth the tribe of Border in days gone by, long before the tribe of Vaughan stuffeth the tribe of Ponting in that great battle known as the Ashes. And the whole family were initiated into the secret ritual of Slippeth, Slappeth, Sloppeth, and all was well.

And behold, as in a vision, Adrian and Bridget were led to the tribe of Redcliffe, where they were booked to doeth their first talk. And Adrian saith unto the Lord, "One small point before we begin. Thinkest thou that – "

And the Lord interrupteth, saying, "Get on with it!"'

Questions: very useful, as long as they are not the kind of focused, cul-de-sac queries you sometimes hear from Bible-study group leaders, as in: 'Now, having read the passage, do we think the leper was pleased or upset to be healed?'

Quinquagenarian: what I am and shall continue to be for not very many more years – look it up for yourself.

Quodlibet: a topic for theological debate. Thus, in a group discussion on the theory of Christian belief one might hear the following piece of dialogue:

A: Would anyone be very upset if I were to bring up a quodlibet?
B: (*horrified and moving with unaccustomed speed*) Can you hang on while I get a bowl from the kitchen?

ROAD TO DAMASCUS

R

Rabbith: (1) one of the towns allocated to the tribe of Issachar in the nineteenth chapter of the book of Joshua (2) pets kept by William Brown's annoying, lisping friend, Violet Elizabeth Bott.

Rabbits: what are rabbits doing in a glossary of Christian terms? You will understand when I tell you about something that happened to me a couple of years ago. It will involve making a dismal confession. I have confessed publicly to all sorts of things in the past, but nothing like this. This dark revelation really does take the biscuit. Actually, it takes the whole of one of those large metal tins of assorted chocolate biscuits with a selection of the sweet pink crunchy ones that I love.

And it wouldn't be so bad if some dramatic sin were involved. An affair with Madonna. Kidnapping the president of the United States. Stealing a million pounds. At least those would be interesting. No, my secret vice is much less dramatic and far more shameful than those things. My confession concerns rabbits. I shall explain.

I catch the train from London to Polegate quite frequently. The journey takes an hour and twenty minutes, and although the countryside passed through by the train is attractive, it has also become very familiar. To make the time pass more quickly I have developed a game that is best played in the late afternoon of a sunny day, because that is when rabbits come out in their greatest numbers.

Oh, dear.

I've started, so I suppose I shall have to finish.

My fantasy game involves earning large, imaginary sums of money as a reward for spotting real rabbits. It works like this. If I see a single rabbit I can claim one thousand pounds. Right? But if I make that claim I can earn nothing more for the rest of the journey. If, however, I decide to continue counting rabbits, I lose my thousand pounds, but I get a further thousand pounds for each sighting until I have spotted ten, at which point I can claim ten thousand pounds. I can then, if I wish, give up my rights to that claim and go for twenty rabbits and twenty thousand pounds. Mind you, both the 'ten' and the 'twenty' totals have to be complete, or I receive nothing. Are you following?

Sometimes, locked into this fantasy, with the train approaching its final destination, my face is pressed to the glass and my whole body rigid and quivering with the desperate need to see just two more rabbits before the rail-side houses of Polegate appear and my prize is won or lost. More than once I have emerged goggle-eyed from this trance-like state to find fellow-passengers gazing at me with alarm, clearly puzzled by the single-minded, passionate urgency with which I have been scrutinising quite ordinary fields and bushes. They have no idea what is at stake, of course. I tend not to explain.

So, there we are. A glimpse of my pathetic inner life. I would never have shared it if this 'thing' hadn't happened a couple of years ago. It spoiled my game. I don't count rabbits any more. This is what happened.

I was sitting on the train, happily earning rabbit money as usual. In fact, I was up to fifteen thousand, and feeling optimistic, especially as the train was fast approaching a spot at the corner of a field near Wivelsfield where rabbits always seemed to gather. I needed five of the creatures to turn up and my twenty thousand would be safe.

'What if each rabbit meant a thousand souls saved for Christ? Would the game work just as well?'

Not a voice. Just a thought. And I have learned to be wary about words that pop into my head, especially when they invite me to dive headlong into a vat of boiling guilt. Bad pseudo-evangelical habits die hard. Nevertheless, I did consider the question as the train chugged towards Haywards Heath. The answer, of course, was no. No, the game would not work so well if each rabbit represented a thousand saved souls. It would be boring. One thousand imaginary saved souls would not warm me up half as much as the notion of one thousand imaginary pounds. The incentive to play my silly game would evaporate.

I didn't bother looking for my missing five rabbits after that. I was feeling sad, and a bit confused. It was not, you understand, that I believed there was anything deeply evil about my ridiculous rabbit game. It was just a fantasy. Fantasy is one of those commonplace things that tend to provoke a negative knee-jerk reaction from some sections of the church, but it certainly has its own part to play in normal, healthy living. I suppose the thing that struck me most forcibly was the realisation of how frequently I do default to the imagined acquisition of material wealth when I need a fantasy to keep me warm. I had never really focused on this before, and it depressed me somewhat.

All bad experiences are potentially divine manure, however, and hopefully this will be no exception. I am terrible at making promises to myself and worse at keeping them, but I shall make a bit of an effort to monitor the components of my fantasy life, and try not to indulge the ones that draw me far, far away from the concept of the person I really want to be.

Meanwhile, the imaginary saved souls still don't do it for me, I'm afraid, and the phantom cash has – well, it has lost its appeal. Train journeys seem a little longer nowadays, but the rabbits will just have to count themselves.

Rainbow: sign of God's promise never to flood the world again. In which case, one has to ask what the poor old residents of Bangladesh have done to annoy the Creator so much.

Raised from the dead: (1) restored to life after physical decease (2) brought up as an Anglican.

Rampart: (1) defensive fortification mentioned in the fourth verse of the ninety-first Psalm (2) bit of a sheep.

Rapture: an experience that will involve the sudden disappearance of the elect, but may leave the vertically challenged in rather bizarre company. One assumes that in the American Bible-belt airlines are careful to ensure that either the pilot or the co-pilot is definitely not a Christian.

Rest: according to Genesis, what God did after six days of creative effort. Needs to be checked, perhaps, by those who have developed a rather severe definition of the term 'rest', and seem to think that the Bible actually says:

> On the seventh day God stopped doing interesting things, wiped the smile off his face, and filled up the whole twenty-four hours with the most tedious, uninspiring activities that he could think of. All for our benefit.

Revelation: fascinating and informative final book of the Bible. When interpreted too literally it suggests that heaven will be a cross between one of Eisenstein's epics, a Ken Russell film and a giant game of Cluedo in which just about everyone did it with a candlestick.

Rick Warren: (1) highly successful author of the widely read and extremely helpful *The Purpose Driven Life* (2) a haystack where lots of rabbits live.

Road to Damascus: unreleased movie in the popular series of films starring Bob Hope and Bing Crosby. This hilarious first century romp features Hope as the zany prophet Paul, with his golden-voiced crooning partner as Ananias the lovable but chicken-hearted messenger of God who comes up with the goods in the end. Songs include *Jen-Jen-Jenny the Gentile* and the hauntingly poignant *I was Saul, now I'm Paul, let me gently down the wall.*

Robinson, John: Anglican bishop and author of *Honest to God,* published in the sixties. In his book Robinson dismissed the ludicrous notion of the Creator as an old man in the sky, explaining that God is in fact the 'Ground of our being.' Of course he is. Now we understand. Thank goodness Bishop Robinson got that all sorted out for us.

Rock of ages: (1) well known hymn which celebrates the security we find in the eternal love of God (2) music produced by the Rolling Stones.

Rood Screen: a wooden or stone carved screen separating the nave and the chancel of a church. Not, as some illiterates have supposed, a video player specially designed for watching blue movies.

STATIONS OF THE CROSS

S

Saint Christopher medal: metal disk usually engraved with a picture of the patron saint of travellers. Often found miraculously unharmed in the burnt out wrecks of vehicles.

Saint John of the Cross: Christian mystic and philosopher whose spiritual experiences are sometimes claimed by modern Christians whose 'Long dark night of the soul' turns out to actually be the 'Short, poorly lit, early evening of the indigestion.' Or the 'Endless, nausea-filled, headache-ridden twenty-four hours of the hangover.'

Salvation: the reason for luring all those people up to the front with the promise of a bacon sandwich. Bacon sandwiches are undoubtedly a matter for serious concern, but they are perhaps not quite in the same league as salvation. God wants as many people as possible to be saved. So do I. So, I expect, do you. But what is it all about? What does it mean to be saved? Saved from what? Saved *for* what? Should the whole business of salvation have a significant impact on my present as well as on my future? Speaking of the future, what can we expect from an eternity spent in heaven? How can we possibly make sense of heaven when our feet remain so solidly on Earth? Where is the interface, the meeting point between the flesh and the Spirit? And when all the strange religious terms and voices and patterns and mantras and man-made conventions have faded away, what will be left?

These are the kinds of questions that I have been asking and attempting to answer for more than twenty years. If you want to know more about those attempts you can bore yourself to death by reading not just the rest of this book, but all my other books as well. They are shot through with passion and puzzlement, and will probably continue to be so until the day I die. If, however, you are anxious to retain your sanity, here is the severely shortened version of what I mistily understand about salvation.

There is one God. He made the world and everything that is in it, including men and women. His plan was for us to live in perfect harmony with him. It was to be a magnificent situation for all concerned. For a while it was. Then something went horribly, dreadfully wrong. Don't bother asking me why an omnipotent, omniscient God should create beings in the full knowledge that they would turn against him. I have no idea, and nor has anybody else. Don't let the frighteningly certain ones tell you otherwise. We understand immeasurably less than a billionth of a trillionth of the truth that lies behind life as we know it. This truly ghastly thing that happened somehow separated human beings from God, who nevertheless continued to love them/us with a passion that is impossible to comprehend. Desperate to heal the rift, he devised a rescue plan. Jesus came to the earth. He was the Son of God. He was additionally, in some mysterious way, God himself. He was also a real man, tempted by the same things as any other human being. He resisted all temptation because he wanted to be obedient to his father. Jesus taught, preached and told stories for three years, until, when he was thirty-three years old, he was executed on a cross by the Romans as a conciliatory gesture to a section of Jewish religious leaders. Three days later he came back to life and was seen by hundreds of people before physically ascending from the earth and disappearing from the sight of his disciples.

Because Jesus was executed on the cross it is now possible for any or all of us, through repentance, baptism and obedience, to recover the magnificent relationship with God that was destroyed in days gone by. There are no easy answers here either. Somehow the gap between us and God; the sin, the breakdown, the catastrophic split, the ruin and decay of all that was supposed to be, has been sorted out. If you and I accept the death and resurrection of Jesus as a living, divine, working mechanism in our own lives we shall one day go home to God and find peace. But because the world is as it is, and because of our individual differences, life on earth will continue to be hard for most of us, as it was for Jesus. The Holy Spirit, sent by Jesus himself after his death, offers support and strength for those who call on him.

Those are the bones of what I believe. For me, the flesh is much more problematic. I am what I am. I feel what I feel. I hurt when I hurt. I sing when there is a song in me. I cannot alter the shape of who I am, other than by being obediently co-operative with the will of God in specific matters. Jesus is at the centre of it all, and he is the one who will save me in the end. He knows that we are weak but willing. He knows that the level of our faith and loyalty and fortitude rises and falls continually, but that is all right. He is going to save you and me, not an edited version of us. Here are the words of a song that I sang in unaccompanied fear and trembling to and about him in public more than fifteen years ago. Every word continues to be true:

People, so many people
They say they know all about you

But I know, I know, oh yes, I know
I know it's not always true

People, thousands of people
They say they've heard so much from you
But I know, I know, oh yes, I just know
I know it's not always true

Jesus, Jesus, I'm sorry
I've done it too
But I know, I know, oh yes, I know
You'll forgive me, you always do

And if a small part of a tenth part
Of a hundredth of what I read of you is true
Then I know, I know, oh, yes, I know
I'll be hearing from you soon

Jesus, Jesus,
I love you, I love you
At least I think I do, I think I do, I'm pretty sure I do
And are you pretty sure you love me too?

Jesus, Jesus,
I love you, I love you
I'm pretty sure I do . . .

Salivation army: members of the congregation just before they're allowed to get their hands on the bacon sandwiches.

Samson: leader of Israel for twenty years. According to the sixteenth chapter of the book of Judges, this muscular hero of the Old Testament died with a great big beam on his face – literally (See also **Jawbone of an ass**).

Sanity: a fundamentally human and therefore divine attribute regarded with deep suspicion and considerable uneasiness by certain sections of the church that have not yet got round to experimenting with it.

Second person of the Trinity: actually Jesus, of course, but subject to continual usurpment by money, buildings, hard work, good works, Myers Briggs, efficient organisation, computers, food, the Bible, church activities, buildings, end-times, principles, ministers, religion, theology, knowledge, ignorance, virtue, celibacy, sex, sexuality, abstinence, party spirit, meetings, soundness, politics, prophecy, fame, talent, tradition, single-issue fanaticism, alcohol and family, to name but a few.

See, he is puffed up: early reference to Mr Blobby in the second chapter of Habakkuk (See also **Habakkuk**).

Seminar: anagram of 'remains'.

Seven by seven: how, at God's command, all the 'clean' animals and every single species of bird were instructed to enter Noah's ark. If you don't believe me, turn to the seventh chapter of Genesis and read it for yourself.

Sex: high on just about everyone's agender.

Sex before and outside marriage: a bad idea because when it gets out of control it can easily lead to dancing.

Shakers: members of an American religious sect who, one assumes from their title, not only wanted to be salt in the world, but had also found a way of distributing it.

She pours herself out for others: she creates an awful lot of unnecessary washing-up for some of the others.

Shepherding – Light: the gentle touch of God through his humble servants. The best church leaders are vulnerable, courageous, obedient, not tied to a personal agenda and willing to let God work in his people as he sees fit.

Signs of the Zodiac: twelve equal parts into which a belt of the heavens limited by lines about eight degrees from the elliptic on each side, including all apparent positions of the sun, moon and planets as known to ancient astronomers, is divided. The ridiculous claim that birth within these signs has some direct effect on human beings and their destinies should be utterly rejected, especially by Librans, who, as we all know, are notoriously sensitive to such influences.

Sin against the Holy Spirit: there is now widespread agreement among scholars and theologians that this is almost certainly either scrumping, or failing to fill the ice-tray after making a cold drink.

Single-issue fanatics: over-focused individuals who are a pain in the neck in any context, but a pain in every part of the body when they draw Christians away from the true priorities of their faith. Single-issue fanatics should beware of eclectic shocks.

666: the mark of the beast. Not a bad score if it was out of a thousand. About the equivalent of a 'C' pass at GCSE. Good try, beast – could do better.

Sound Christians: doctrinally accurate believers. An admirable thing to be, of course, but if Jesus were to return once more in the flesh and had to spend some time in hospital, he might guiltily opt to be visited by one or two of those ragged believers who may be a little less sound, but love him, have a pleasant bedside manner, tell some good jokes and don't solemnly consume the grapes they've brought that were supposed to be for him.

Speaking the truth in love: truly wretched business that should only ever be undertaken by those who don't enjoy doing it. Heaven preserve us from the ones who adore every second.

Spirit of heaviness: phenomenon detected in hitherto perfectly happy congregations by church leaders who lose their confidence halfway through a meeting or service.

Spiritual assurance: an inner confidence shared by all Spirit-filled Christians – isn't it? Well, I thought it was. I could be wrong. Maybe it's not. Sometimes I'm absolutely sure it is. At other times I have these

A B C D E F G H I J K L M N O P Q R S T U V W X Y Z

nagging doubts. Mind you, I'm one hundred percent convinced that we all ought to have it – well, perhaps not quite a hundred percent . . .

Spiritual insight: wonderful when it's genuine, most irritating when it's not. As a teenager I once dragged myself to church with flu on Sunday, only to be asked if it really was flu, or whether it was the result of me stepping outside the Lord's will in some way. This rewrite of a famous old Methodist hymn is for all those who have been through the same experience:

And can it be, that no one was concerned
When I staggered in with an awkward lurch
If they had asked me they might have learned
I came off my bike on the way to church
My chain came off
I swerved into a tree
I smashed my shin
And grazed my knee
My chain, my chain came off . . .

Standing on the promises: (1) believing by an act of the will that God is bound to honour the promises he makes in the Bible (2) no wonder we couldn't find them (3) some of us need to be reminded that it is physically impossible to lift any object that we are standing on.

Stations of the cross: (1) series of images or pictures representing the events in Christ's passion before which devotions are performed in some churches (2) places where frustrated commuters wait for trains that are not only late, but lack sufficient carriages to seat all the passengers who need to travel.

Statutory standing prayer posture for bearded Christian male (taken from *The Official Handbook of Christian Postures and Practices,* Chapter three, Section six): the left arm should be placed in a horizontal position across the diaphragm, in such a way that the left hand can be utilised for support of the right elbow. Correctly positioned this will allow the thumb and forefinger of the right hand to be spread widely apart in order to accommodate the slightly projected chin of the bearded praying person, whose head must be inclined downwards at an angle of approximately fifteen degrees from the vertical. If the posture is correct the lower cheeks will be pressed upwards towards the cheekbones. Facial expression should be one of concentrated listening, the eyes closed but not screwed tightly shut. Sensitive, mildly surprised twitches of the eyebrows and a limited bobbing motion of the upper body are permissible, but should not detract from the general air of one who is in direct and serious contact with the divine intelligence (Caution: for obvious reasons this posture should not be adopted by those without beards).

Strive: (1) something we don't do. We are taught that we don't do it. We must just grit our teeth and not do it. It's simply a matter of effort and will. *Don't do it.* Whatever you do, don't strive! Come on; put your backs into it for goodness sake! Not striving doesn't happen all on its own, you know. Just get on with it! All those who need to stop striving – ready, steady, go! (2) applies in the secular world just as much. One well known song by an even better known gravel-voiced singer might be rendered in the following form:

I am straining, I am spraining
All the muscles in my throat
I'm not joking, I'm damn near choking
It gets worse with every note

Can you hear me? Don't come near me
Keep your distance, stay away
It's not rejection, it's infection
You might catch it, who can say?

'Charlton Heston kept his vest on'
That's what mum said day and night
She'd rebuke us, now this mucus
Is suggesting she was right

All my charm's gone, Louis Armstrong's
Like a choirboy compared with this
Folks who hear me never cheer me
All they do is boo and hiss

I am straining, I am spraining
All the muscles in my throat
I'm not joking, I'm damn near choking
It gets worse with every note.

Subculture: (1) social ethos on board the Nautilus (2) a cultural group within a larger group, often having beliefs or interests at variance with those of the larger culture. Aspects of the evangelical subculture are apparent in this fresh presentation of a familiar chorus:

Father God I wonder
how I managed to exist
without an NIV concordance
and a Harvest Praise CD

I have been a member of
the EA since November
Roger Forster lives inside me
and it's just as though he's here beside me

I'll hide every stumble
I'll quote Nicky Gumbel
I'll be proudly humble, for evermore
I will fake ecstatic
role-play charismatic
I will be dogmatic, but never sure.

Superstition: widely held but unjustified idea of the effects or nature of a thing. A common phenomenon in human beings generally, and a substitute for spiritual common sense in the lives of more than a few Christians. Exemplified by the tendency to ascribe the direct intervention of God to random coincidences between prayer and experience, and to ignore the occasions when there is no such correlation. The devil has always been on hand with buckets full of false pearls to pour over and obscure examples of the profoundly valuable genuine article. The verses that follow demonstrate just how silly it can get:

I drove to town this morning, it wasn't very far,
But all the way I asked myself where I would park the car.
Imagine my amazement when, in Devonshire Parade,
I found the perfect parking space,
Gosh, I wish I'd prayed!

In April at Spring Harvest our chalet was complete,
Except that towels were not supplied, we'd have to use a sheet.

My chalet-mate said, 'Problem solved, my son's come to our aid,
His car was stacked with extra towels!'
How we wished we'd prayed!

We planned a parish picnic for a day in late July,
Hoping that in summertime the weather would be dry.
When I awoke to cloudy skies and rain I was dismayed,
But just in time the sun came out!
Damn, I wish I'd prayed!

Synods in England and Scotland: (See **Never Never Land**)

T

Tarshish: (1) place from which Jonah set sail when he disobeyed God's command to go to Nineveh (2) Paul's birthplace, as pronounced by an Ephesian who has rejected the apostle's more spiritual option of being drunk in the Spirit.

The first Noel: (1) Christmas carol about the announcement of the birth of Jesus to the shepherds (2) just as annoying when he arrived on radio and television in the Sixties as the re-invented one who now presents *Deal or No Deal* on Channel 4.

The Lord will bring the ones he wants: desperate phrase sometimes employed by those responsible for a badly organised, poorly advertised, underfinanced,

A B C D E F G H I J K L M N O P Q R S T U V W X Y Z

low quality Christian event for which only thirteen tickets have been sold in total.

The pits: (1) the lowest and worst point or condition that can be reached (2) what Jesus is in the great motor-race of life.

The quick and the dead: (1) those alive and those who have passed on (2) front and back rows respectively in your average High Street church.

The Righteous Brothers: stage act worked on privately by Jesus and James probably at Mary's suggestion, as something to fall back on if the day jobs didn't work out in the end. Jesus would do tricks with fish and coins and vats of water and wine and tell a few stories. James would do some of his classic stand-up material, such as asking a member of the audience if they believed in God and then saying 'Well done – so do the devils!', or miming walking past a suffering person and calling out 'Bless you!' as he went by. Good material, a lot of talent and some great ideas, but management had other ideas.

The ruler of the kingdom of the air: (1) Satan, as described in the second chapter of Ephesians (2) Terry Wogan?

Theology: (1) the systematic study of theistic, and especially Christian, religion (2) anagram of 'O get holy!'

There was a real sense of the presence of God: statement frequently made by those who have found themselves in a peaceful place or a situation where it is possible to be temporarily distracted from personal pressures. For some reason God seems to reveal his presence much less in places like crowded supermarkets, bus queues, traffic jams, centre aisles of aircraft while you're waiting to get off, awkward interviews with bank managers and the last half hour of putting three small children to bed on your own. Seems odd that he should absent himself at times like this, when his presence would be most appreciated. Is it possible that we have failed to understand what the presence of God really means? Surely not . . .

Third World needs: one of those boring topics that continually threaten to spoil the peaceful enjoyment of our faith.

Those who have ears to hear: expression used by Jesus in connection with listening to the voice of the Spirit. Some of us have a bit of a problem with this. There have been times when I have failed even to hear the voice of a simple sheet of instructions.

There was, for example, the time when I had been invited to speak at an ecumenical event that began with a two-mile walk. It was a short pilgrimage. In a couple of hours' time, when everyone had assembled at our destination, I would be speaking to the several hundred people who were expected to attend. I had been placed right at the front of the procession, just at the rear of the cross bearer, in the centre of a little knot of church leaders representing the wide variety of denominations that were involved in the day.

Behind us streamed a veritable river of people of all types and ages. It was quite a fine day, and there was a lot of contented chatter as we walked, until, after we had progressed about a mile and a half, and just as I was beginning to express strong views on some topic that seemed terribly important to me, I became aware that everyone else had stopped talking, and that mine was literally the only voice to be heard.

I really did feel immensely flattered. This close attention to my views was quite unprecedented. I could only suppose that I must have hit on a rare vein of brilliance.

'And,' I caught myself thinking, 'let's face it, these people around me are highly intelligent churchmen.'

I stole a glance at them. They were walking along in silence, heads bowed, clearly fascinated by every word that was coming out of my mouth. I raised my voice a little so that more people in the procession would be able to enjoy and benefit from my wisdom. It seemed unfair that those farther back should miss out.

Even as these thoughts were passing through my mind, I noticed one strange thing about the man who was walking along on my right hand side. The expression on his face seemed to be twitching to and fro between irritation and polite interest in a most peculiar fashion.

'Perhaps,' I conjectured, 'he is just the teeniest bit jealous of my newly emerged conversational skills.'

Well, that was understandable, I generously conceded. He was a brother, and must be forgiven and respected.

It was then, quite abruptly, and with a thrill of sheer horror, that I remembered a line from the leaflet that had been given out to us all to read before we began our walk.

'The final half mile of the walk will be used for silent prayer and contemplation. Please respect the needs of others in this matter.'

My face flamed like a fiery furnace. The silence that had descended was not one that signified close attention to my voice and views. It had nothing to do with me at all. Brilliant? Oh, no. I was not brilliant, just stupid. I had gone on loudly bleating my half-baked views on whatever silly subject it was, long after everyone else had obediently moved into silent prayer and contemplation. I had signally failed to respect the needs of others in this matter. And, of course, this man beside me, being one of the others, was squirming, not with envy, but with embarrassment and annoyance because I was not respecting his needs. He had wanted me to shut up, but feared that he might offend me if he said anything.

I employed what was left of my time of prayer and silent contemplation in pleading with heaven that the ground beneath my feet would be allowed to open up and swallow me, but God in his infinite wisdom did not answer my prayer. I could not find it in my heart to blame him. I fancied that, by now, he was beginning to rather enjoy the situation.

'Why is it,' I asked God, 'that there are so many rough places to fall into and trip over when you try to follow Jesus?'

It may have more to do with where you choose to place your size-twelve feet; I seemed to hear him reply.

I asked myself if I would ever relate this embarrassing little story to anyone else. The answer was yes, probably, but not for a while.

I seem to make an idiot of myself on a fairly regular basis, but I am afraid there is no secretly interesting and virtuous basis for it. I'm just an idiot sometimes. I thank God for keeping me safely in his family, and putting up with me, and smiling at me, and encouraging me to keep going, and finding opportunities for me to work for Him, knowing full well that I am likely to make a whole set of completely new mistakes . . .

Three wise men: (1) endless magic on the road to Bethlehem (2) wise enough to locate Jesus, but not wise enough to keep their mouths shut when they met Herod.

Thus saith the Lord: not before putting his teeth back in, he doesn't.

Tithing: practice of giving a tenth of one's income for the work of God. Postponed for a couple of millennia in most church communities while we continue to attempt to sort out the knotty problem of whether this means ten per cent of net or gross income.

Tittle: Jot's straight man. Never managed to make it on his own after Jot overdid it and was forced to retire (See also **Jot**).

Treachery: terrible sin of betrayal and disloyalty in which people are metaphorically stabbed in the back. A great comfort to know that, in the Christian world, we can at least depend on being stabbed in the front.

Trinity: the Christian Godhead, Father, Son and Holy Spirit, three persons in one. Not, as the ancient heresy of modalism suggests, one person with three functions. The Trinity is not like those carpet cleaners which claim to beat as they sweep as they clean.

Triumph Herald: (1) car model that was very popular a few decades ago (2) Graham Kendrick.

Triumphalist: the equivalent, in hiking terms, of the one with big leg muscles who strides ahead at great speed making a lot of noise about how easy it is, forgetting that others have to stay at the back helping the slow ones and the ones whose shoelaces need tying and the fat ones and the lame ones and the ones who are beginning to wish they'd never started in the first place.

Truth: a desirable quality for Christians, but virtually indefinable and as slippery as a bar of soap. Worth persevering with, though, as the following dialogue suggests:

A: I've been thinking about that marvellous verse, John 8:32. You know the one I mean?

B: (*after an infinitesimal pause*) Yeah. Yes, of course. Oh, marvellous! Wonderful, wonderful verse.
A: (*thrilled and a little surprised*) Oh, great! You know it. So what is it that's special to you about that verse?
B: Er, well, it – I suppose it's er the way in which, you know, God er speaks through the words in the er the words in the er verse . . .
A: (*enthralled*) Right! And what exactly do you feel he's saying to you?
B: Hmm. He says er – he's saying er he's conveying the essence of the real meaning of er the heart of the centre of the er message of the – the verse.
A: (*genuinely interested*) Which is what?
B: Sorry – what, what, what?
A: What is the centre of the message?
B: Ah, right! Sorry, I see what you mean. Well, yeah, mmm, okay. Yeah! The centre of the message is basically that we should all – all of us – we should all, we should all do it. We should all erm take it on board.
A: Take what on board?
B: The message.
A: Which is – what?
B: You know, it's just occurred to me – translations do differ a lot. How does yours actually put it – I mean the exact wording?
A: Well, what's the wording of yours?
B: (*finally giving up*) Oh, dear, you get yourself into so much trouble if you don't tell the truth.
A: Oh, well yours must be a very modern version. In mine Jesus just says, 'The truth will set you free.'
B: Aaah, yes, of course. Do you know, I think he may well be right.

UR

U

Umbilical cord: flexible cordlike structure attaching the foetus to the placenta which is cut after a person is born. Not to be confused with the 'Unbiblical cord', which is severed when a person is born for the second time.

Unity: the bond that automatically joins together all those who love Jesus. Definitely not an informal agreement that we all hate the Baptists. It is easy to believe that we are more unified than is actually the case. Witness the following discussion between two people from widely differing denominations who have met to plan a joint service:

A: When you think about it this is amazing, isn't it?
B: What's that, then?
A: Well, that you and I, two people from very different denominations are able to meet like this to plan a joint service. I mean, let's face it, we wouldn't have been able to agree on anything ten years ago.
B: True, that's true – well, nearer fifteen.
A: Oh, I was actually going to say it's probably less than ten.
B: I'm pretty sure it's at least fifteen.
B: (*about to say more*) I don't – well, around ten, anyway.
B: Yeah, I suppose it could be a little bit less than fifteen.
A: Anyway. (*produces clipboard*) I've taken the liberty of jotting down a few ideas at home just to get us started.
B: Have you? Oh, yes. Oh, good. Oh, that's good. You've just – jotted a few ideas down.
A: Yes, is that all right?
B: Fine. Fine. Yes, that's fine. Few ideas – yes, that's fine.
A: Good. Right, well I thought we could start with a prayer.
B: (*almost imperceptible*) Hm!
A: Sorry – what?
B: I didn't say anything.
A: Yes, you did. You said (*an exact imitation*) 'Hm!'
B: Did I? Oh, I was just interested that you thought we should start the whole thing off with a prayer, that's all. Just – found that interesting.

A: So, are you saying you're not happy for us to start with a prayer?
B: Oh, no, no, a prayer's absolutely fine. Absolutely fine. (*pause*) Or a hymn.
A: Ri-i-ight, now, by a hymn, presumably you mean a song.
B: Do I?
A: Well, we tend to call them songs nowadays.
B: Oh, do we?
A: Yes, we think hymns – hymns – sounds a bit, sort of, old-fashioned and kind of stuffy.
B: Oh, I see. Old-fashioned. Stuffy.
A: Yes, you know the sort of thing I mean. (*laughs*) Like that hymn you lot sing about falling off your bike.
B: Falling off your bike?
A: Yes, you know the one I mean. (*sings*)
My chain came off.
I swerved into a tree,
I smashed my shin, I bashed my chin,
I grazed my knee.
My chain, my chain came off –
B: Yes, all right, all right! Well, what about your songs, then? What about
The name of the Lord is
A strong tower,
The righteous run into it
And bang their heads.
A: (*suddenly serious*) Now you are verging on irreverence.
B: No, I'm not, I'm Church of England.
A: Oh, really! (*sighs*) Well, anyway, I thought we could have one song after the prayer, and –

B: You mean this prayer you want to have right at the beginning of the service?
A: Er, the beginning of the meeting, yes –
B: Beginning of the service, right.
A: Meeting. And then maybe another one just before the message.
B: Sorry, just before the what?
A: Just before the message.
B: Message? Message from whom to whom? About what?
A: You know, the message, the message, the message, the message, the talk.
B: Oh, you mean the sermon.
A: Well, I suppose you could call it that.
B: Well, we do call it that.
A: Yes, well, we call it – the message.
B: (*almost under his breath*) And we call it the sermon.
A: Anyway, what I'm suggesting is that we have the second song followed by the message, and then –
B: You know, it's just occurred to me, you ought to combine the song and the message. You could call it – the 'sausage.'
A: Ah, well, now you're being what we call 'silly.'
B: Oh, we don't call it 'silly.'
A: What do you call it?
B: We call it nonconformist.
A: Now that is just plain insulting!
B: Sorry. I'm sorry, no, I am sorry.
A: Look, perhaps we should talk about the confession.

B: The confession. Yes, all right, perhaps we should.
A: Well, I think the confession ought to come quite near the beginning of the meeting – er service.
B: Right. Just after the first hymn – I mean – song?
A: Yes, and quite a long way before the mess – er...
B: The talk?
A: Yes, well before the talk. Good. See! Now we're getting somewhere. Right, so where are we going to put the time of sharing gifts?
B: (*puzzled pause*) Er it's not a Christmas service, is it?
A: No, not those kinds of gifts. Spiritual gifts. Tongues and prophecy. You know the sort of thing. For instance, I might suddenly have a word for you.
B: I see. What – like 'song', you mean? Or 'meeting'?
A: No, not that sort of word. A message from the Lord.
B: Oh, you've arranged for God to do the sermon, have you?
A: You know that's not what I mean.
B: Sorry – sorry – sorry . . .
A: Right, just a couple more things. Do we want to include gathering at the Lord's Table?
B: (*pause*) Well, yes, fine, I don't mind, as long as it leaves time for communion.
A: (*sighs*) It's exactly the same thing, as you well know!

A: (*that's it*) Actually, no. No it's not. It's not the same thing at all. Communion is about people reverentially taking bread and wine from silver platters and chalices, whereas gathering at blah, blah, blah whatever you said is about someone giving out little piddling glasses of weak cherryade to people who can't be bothered to get off their bums and come to the front.
B: (*gloves off*) Oh, it is, is it? Let me tell you the people in our church do not have – bums. They have bottoms! Let's talk about something you lot do, shall we? The exchanging of the Peace. Let's talk about that. That precious little moment of so-called informality when everybody freezes with fear and can't make up their minds who to kiss, who to hug, who to shake hands with or who to smack in the mouth. Exchanging the Peace! Huh! It ought to be called passing on the – the – tension!
A: Oh, really! Well, at least we don't do that silly, sippy, sicky, smirking over your shoulder ghastly gooey saying the grace to each other thing.
B: At least our ministers don't dress like pregnant women.
A: Some of our ministers are pregnant women! At least we don't make a big stupid thing about inviting the Holy Spirit in.
B: Ah, that would explain why he's never there, then, wouldn't it?
A: Anyway (*running out of ideas*) you've got big ears!
B: They have to be to pick up what's coming out of your huge fat mouth!

A: You know nothing!
B: You don't!
A: You don't!
B: You don't!
A: You don't!
B: You don't!
A: You don't!
(*slightly embarrassed pause*)
B: So, how are we doing, then?
A: Fine, I think. Erm, presumably we'll invite everyone to our event.
B: Well, I did think perhaps – not the Presbyterians.
A: (*after a pause*) Do you know, I am so glad you said that.
B: Well, there are, you know –
BOTH: Limits.
B: There are limits, aren't there?
A: There are, there really are.
BOTH: Presbyterians
(*they both shake their heads in agreement*)
B: (*sighs*) Isn't unity wonderful?
A: Wonderful!
B: You know what? It's only the details that separate us.
A: Absolutely! Well, not *just* the details – sorry, sorry . . .

Universalist: (1) a person who holds that all of mankind will eventually be saved (2) anagram of 'Elvis is a turn' and 'salient virus.'

Unprogressive Anglican Church: one in which the congregation has not split yet.

Unsaved: (1) not redeemed by the death and resurrection of Jesus (2) any ball kicked diagonally from a long way out into the net above and behind ex-England goalkeeper David Seaman's head.

Ur: famous city on the Euphrates in south Babylonia, created by God to make life easier for modern crossword compilers.

A B C D E F G H I J K L M N O P Q R S T U V W X Y Z

VERSIONS OF THE BIBLE

Valiant: we are reliably informed by John Bunyan that he who would be this should basically begin by coming hither.

Vehicle: feature of an over-used metaphor in which it is proposed that each Christian is a car and the Bible is the manufacturer's manual. More accurately, most of us feel that we are the self-assembly dressing-table kit, and the Bible is the MFI sheet of instructions.

Versions of the Bible: space to mention only a few here:
(1) King James Version: form in which the Bible was originally written in seventeenth century English.

Later translated into Hebrew and Greek for some obscure reason, and then translated back again into those ridiculous modern English versions. As to whether thou believest this or nay, verily thou must surely decideth for thine self.

(2) Good News Bible: version preferred by those who are fed up with the bad news that clutters up all the other translations.

(3) Good News for Modern Man: seriously negative vibes for anyone who didn't make it past the nineteen-fifties.

(4) Digest Bible: the one where your name is actually mentioned in print throughout the New Testament, and there is a chance to win your salvation in a special draw that is to be decided immediately before the Second Coming.

(5) The Living Bible: (a) a version of Scripture which has angered some Christian folk. Very understandable, because it makes the mistake of enabling readers to easily understand what the original writers were trying to say. The very idea of this is, of course, quite unacceptable and totally against the spirit of Scripture (b) a useful antidote to The Comatose Bible.

(6) The Readers' Bible: uses the novel device of printed words on the page instead of the usual Morse code, semaphore or Egyptian hieroglyphics.

(7) New International Version: ideal for those who are not happy with the plethora of decrepit, very local translations of Scripture.

(8) Red letter Bible: specially designed for the use of communist landlords.

(9) Amplified Bible: can be read aloud in churches of any size without having to use a sound system.

(10) New English Bible: a refreshing change from that ancient foreign rubbish.
(11) The 'Living, throbbing, slides along the pew, opens itself at random and points out a verse specially meant for you' version: invented by me, but nevertheless used by a number of people I know quite regularly.

Very bad beginnings: distorted, negative experiences of religious behaviour that can have serious long-term effects on those who start their Christian lives under the wrong leadership.

In this connection, my mind goes back to the man who was my junior school class teacher for a year when I was nine or ten years old. He rejoiced in the unusual name of Mr Bung. Actually, that statement is far from accurate. He did not rejoice in it. He was not a rejoicing person. He did not rejoice in anything. More specifically, there were two things that this man clearly loathed. One was being a teacher, and the other, as far as we knew or could guess, was any and every single child between the ages of nine and ten that he had encountered in the course of his career; the very age group, in fact, that he must have been dealing with on a daily basis for years.

Mr Bung – I find it hard to believe that he ever had a Christian name, I suppose he must have done, although we never learned what it was – was a balding, irascible, square-spectacled little man with a monk-like tonsure, who kept three canes standing in the corner of his classroom, each one about two and a half feet long.

Grotesquely, he had christened each of them with a human name. One, the stoutest, was called Sir Ben Dover. Gettit? Another, slightly less stout, was known as Sir Percy Vere. The third, and by far the whippiest and most venomous of the trio in my painful experience, had been christened Clarence by Mr Bung. We all dreaded the evil Clarence.

In an age when corporal punishment was allowed to be administered at the teacher's discretion, Mr Bung wielded all three of his canes with enormous gusto on quite a number of occasions during the year that I was in his class. Clarence was reserved for the worst and most obdurate cases. Looking back, I can see that there were times when some of us little boys, usually the 'stupid' ones, were literally beaten up. Again in retrospect, I suspect very strongly that the degree of gusto involved was not limited to the seriousness of the offence that was being punished. I think, on reflection, that this man who was responsible for educating us and nurturing our young lives rather enjoyed beating children. He was an odd person.

One of the few things we did enjoy in this twentieth century Dickensian's class was singing. Our teacher played the piano with tightly contained fury, as though the keys that made up each chord were a clutch of annoying little boys. This gave his accompaniment a vigorous, rattling, staccato urgency that we enjoyed enormously. Songs such as *Riding Down from Bangor, Camptown Races, The Raggle-taggle*

Gypsies and other classics that no one sings any more nowadays were contained in a printed song book with floppy pages that was given out, one between two boys, at the beginning of each music lesson. We loved every moment of these opportunities for vocal release, singing lustily and loudly, enjoying the sense that the vigorous use of our voices was, for once, being adjudged a good thing.

One day, wildly daring, a few of us who sat near the back of the room decided to sing our own small-boyishly scurrilous versions of lines in one or two of the songs. Remembering what a martinet this horrible little man was, I simply cannot imagine how we thought we could possibly get away with this. You never, never messed Mr Bung about. He had a Regimental Sergeant Major's eye for even the most miniscule item of disarray in the uniform of our good behaviour. Why did we do it? It was ever so with little boys, I suppose. The danger itself was a delicious element in the temptation. The fact is that we did it, and to our amazement, we did seem to be getting away with this sin of sins. We sang our terribly naughty version of selected lines and verses at a slightly reduced volume, but with a relish that we fondly imagined to be concealed. One or two other, more timid souls, joined in with the fun as they realised that, what we might nowadays describe as the muppet-like figure at the piano, had failed to register our pernicious behaviour. Later, out on the yard at playtime, we congratulated each other with wild whoops and swinging smacks on the back. With our immense cunning and cleverness we had succeeded in deceiving our infamously eagle-eyed teacher.

Alas, we had underestimated Mr Bung. We had underestimated his powers of detection, and we had seriously underestimated his capacity for taking and enjoying a more delayed and subtle revenge than was afforded by the three canes that, every day, leered expectantly at us like a gang of skinny, thuggish enforcers from the corner next to the upright piano.

Two days later another singing session was scheduled, straight after morning assembly. Songbooks were given out, Mr Bung seated himself behind the piano, his hands in their familiar rigid strangling postures descended onto the keys, and soon we were lifting the classroom ceiling off with *Riding Down from Bangor,* one of our all-time favourites. We always loved singing that song out with as high a decibel level as our healthy young lungs could manage. This time was no exception. We gave it everything we had. The sound made by Mr Bung's class that morning must have been audible in the next county. We really rocked!

'Riding down from Bangor on an eastern train,
After weeks of hunting in the woods of – '

Abruptly, without warning, the accompaniment stopped. The lid of the battered old upright piano slammed shut with a sound like thunder, and, like a vengeful little god, Mr Bung rose ominously to his feet, his square, pinched face a mask of satisfaction and malice as it appeared like an evil gargoyle over the top of the piano. As the last treble voice faded into troubled silence, we waited fearfully. As far as we were concerned he might as well have been donning the black cap.

'Last time we had a singing lesson,' he announced in his snapping, rat-trap of a voice, 'some of you silly little boys thought it was very funny to sing the wrong words to these songs. Hands up all those who thought it was funny to change the words of the songs.'

In the absence of heroes, lunatics and suicidally courageous comedians, this was never going to happen in Mr Bung's class. Our arms might as well have been limp sticks of celery.

'None of you. Good!'

'Good' was clearly exactly what it was not.

'Our last singing lesson showed me something,' he continued. 'What it showed me is that we need to do some work on remembering what the words of the songs are supposed to be.' Pause. 'Does anyone want to tell me that I'm wrong?'

He glared challengingly from terrified face to terrified face. Eyes flickered nervously from Mr Bung to the three canes in the corner and back again. In the case of some of us, breath was sucked through clenched teeth as the memory of past pain filled even our hardboiled young minds with ghastly anticipation. It would have been easier to strike a match on jelly than to put a hand up and tell Mr Bung that he was wrong.

A B C D E F G H I J K L M N O P Q R S T U V W X Y Z

'Right, well in that case – Robert!'

Robert was a pale, thin lad who sat at the front of the class. Despite being a chronically well behaved, tidy and highly achieving boy, he lived in a state of constant, quivering fear. On hearing his name called he twitched convulsively like an electrocuted bunny and turned the colour of decaying tripe.

'Yes, sir!' he gulped.

'Hand out that pile of rough paper that's lying on my desk. You can all spend the whole morning, including playtime, copying out the correct words of the songs from the book, and you can do it in silence. Any boy who speaks or slacks will be severely caned.'

Sir Percy, Sir Ben and the abominable Clarence seemed to lick their lips in fiendish anticipation.

It was a calculatedly cruel punishment. Mr Bung must have been planning it and thinking about it and enjoying it in anticipation for more than forty-eight hours. The wrenching, dislocating shock of finding our enjoyment transmuted into fear and mindless toil in such an unexpected manner did funny things to our insides. It did to mine, anyway. And an entire morning spent in silence engaged on a task that was pointless but had to be done with meticulous neatness to avoid further punishment – well, for your average healthy nine or ten-year-old, that was punishment indeed. I don't think we ever sang the wrong words to the songs again.

My experience of Mr Bung caused a nervousness that was a part of my life for an inordinate length of time when I was a child. My encounter with his ghastly teaching methods was so intense and overwhelming, and his power over us so absolute, that my juvenile concept of the nature of education was branded with his mark, as it were. That was how teachers behaved, and that was how life in a classroom was lived. So strong was this conviction that it survived for two troubled years during which I had teachers who were much more benevolent and constructive than Mr Bung. When would my new, apparently nice teachers reveal that they were just like Mr Bung after all? At which point would they stop the music and force us into doing pointless, onerous tasks for hour upon hour? Where were the canes hidden? What was the catch?

Later, it came as something of a surprise to wake suddenly to the realisation that Mr Bung had been an unpleasant, sadistic man who should never have been allowed anywhere near children. He was the worst possible example of a teacher and the ethos of his classroom had been inimical to learning and happiness. Knowing these things to be true, I was finally free to believe that there was another way of teaching and being taught, and Mr Bung was reduced to the status of a faint, haunting presence in some distant corner of my mind.

As I said earlier the whole thing is somewhat reminiscent of problems that some Christians encounter in connection with their churches. Not, I hasten to add, that the organisation of any modern church organisations or systems can be compared to Mr Bung's classroom regime. Good gracious, no! Let us be realistic. Why, in the latter case we are talking about a group of tightly controlled human beings who were discouraged from individual expression and thought, got told off if they so much as put a toe over the line and were subject to one man's obsessional view of the way things were, with a constant threat of guilt and punishment if they dared to disagree or try to change anything. There aren't any churches like that, are there?

Seriously, although many believers have wonderful experiences of being nurtured in good churches, there are people, and my wife and I have met a good number of them, who have the same problem with their personal history of church life as I had with getting Mr Bung's distorted model of education out of my head. Ideas that were taught, the attitude of the minister, the atmosphere of worship, stated and unstated restraints that dictated behaviour, the style of prayer, areas of encouragement and discouragement, social mores of a specific denomination or sub-denomination, all or any of these components can burn themselves into the hearts of vulnerable Christians and leave them incapable of accommodating other, different concepts of Christian worship and life without suffering from debilitating, destructive guilt.

When every spiritual instinct in us is demanding that we go against the authority and received wisdom of the religious system or denomination or specific church or any other group that has rigidly defined reality for us, we may become nervously aware that, for the frightened child in us, any such difference of opinion seems like an argument with God himself.

The Son of God does not frighten children, and he is undoubtedly the leader we must follow. It can be very difficult to move on. I have seen such pain in the eyes of those who know that their master is calling them out of an environment or a set of attitudes or a point of view that is not good for them. I understand it. Human beings do so need to belong, and it can be deeply disturbing to leave even a situation in which we are being abused. At least we had a place there. We were part of it. Now the Lord is calling us out to a place where we have never been, and we have no idea where he intends to lead us. Nevertheless, if we are sure that we have heard his voice, we must go. Jesus is not like Mr Bung, and the best place for us to be, however alien it may seem before and after we arrive, is out there on the edge with him.

Vice: (1) something that clamps tight shut and squeezes whatever it is gripping into a different shape (2) something that clamps tight shut and squeezes whoever it is gripping into a different shape.

Virgin berth: a donkey, and then a pile of straw.

Virgin birth: (1) fundamental tenet of the Christian faith concerning the supernatural parenthood of Jesus (2) Richard Branson business initiative that offers easy and attractively priced access to a national midwifery service.

Volunteers: people who never have to worry about waiting around for ages in queues.

WALLS OF JERICHO

Walls of Jericho: (1) fell down after people marched round them and blew rams' horn trumpets at them for seven days in a row. Hard not to sympathise with the walls (2) early ice-cream and sausage firm.

War in heaven: (1) description in Revelation 12:7 of conflict between the archangel Michael and his angels, and the great dragon called the devil, or Satan, and his forces. At the end of the war, Satan and his angels were defeated and hurled to the earth (2) Friday night punch-up in an Indian restaurant.

Weapons of mass destruction: tracts expressing antipathy towards Roman Catholicism.

Welsh revival: could possibly happen, but a long hard climb since the disappearance of great players like Gareth Edwards and J.P.R. Williams.

We're not into playing the numbers game: all efforts to increase the size of our congregation have failed.

We shall be coming back to that point later on: phrase provoking near homicidal rage in long-suffering congregations when used by preachers just as it was looking as if they really might be on the verge of stopping.

When I survey: (1) favourite hymn of Christian architects (2) a truly beautiful and moving hymn, but meaningless if the feelings and thoughts that arise from it are not translated into action of some sort. In that case the first verse might as well go like this:

When I survey the wondrous cross
On which the Prince of glory died
I calculate my profit and loss
And put an extra pound aside.

Whited sepulchre: opprobrious epithet hurled at the Pharisees by Jesus, and yet another warning against the dangers of allowing oneself to be carried away by emulsion.

Why did Jesus say we should 'jam the way the truth and the life?: puzzled question from a child in our church who had been staring solemnly at a banner whose creator had made her 'I' look far too much like a 'J'. Conjures up a fascinating picture of Christians blocking the roads as they loudly claim a monopoly on the truth and actually live life abundantly as the Bible suggests we should. Maybe she got the letter right after all.

William Barclay: fine biblical commentator who, though deceased for many years, still manages to preach his best points all over Great Britain every Sunday.

Witchcraft: (1) the use of magic or sorcery (2) a broom.

Witnessing: something that is supposed to actually draw people to Jesus, but can go horribly wrong, as the following account demonstrates:

It was late summer, and the car in which I was a passenger was making its way to the village where I was due to speak in about two hours. The event was an open-air gathering of representatives from all the local churches in that rural part of the Midlands, and I was excited about this, but I was even more excited by the fact that my friend Arthur had agreed to drive me to the meeting in his car.

Arthur was one of my oldest and dearest friends. I had known him for years, and I loved him quite as much as if he was a member of my family. Fifteen years earlier, when I was suffering from a stress illness, Arthur had become very angry about the way that one or two of the local Christians responded to my problems. Unlike those who were consistently supportive and helpful, these individuals came to my house and shouted loudly about the fact that I must have stepped outside the Lord's will, or demanded that I pull myself together and represent the triumphant, healing power of Jesus. After one or two of these starkly unhelpful visits my wife instituted a front-door filtering process, but Arthur, who was not a Christian, never forgot the virulence with which these hard words had been spoken. He was even more indignant, when, a couple of years later, my second book started to sell in significantly large numbers, and suddenly the church at large wanted me to come and make them laugh and speak to them about what had happened to me. Arthur was deeply cynical and scathing about this apparent hypocrisy. I tried to talk to him about the need to bear in mind the frailty that we all suffer from, but it made no difference.

Our relationship continued as before, but my friend was, if anything, further away from involvement in the church than he had been before my illness. It hurt me. I wanted Arthur to meet Jesus, but he absolutely refused to have anything to do with formal or informal Christian gatherings.

He knew what those people were like, thank you very much, without having to go and actually meet them, so it was much better if he stayed away. That was his position and he was not going to budge from it.

That is why I was so pleased (and rather surprised as well) that he was driving me to this event today. There would be one or two other speakers besides myself, but what I was really hoping was that Arthur would meet ordinary, pleasant Christians, and that these encounters might begin the process of turning around his fixed view of the church in general. At the moment he was wary, but he was here in the car with me, and soon we would be arriving at our destination.

As our little lane met a large roundabout we realised that the queue of cars in the exit that we needed to take must all be going to the ecumenical event as well. It took nearly half an hour to travel less than a mile, but at last we reached the centre of the village and discovered that stewards in yellow over-vests were directing the long line of traffic into two huge open areas accessed by a lane that ran between thatched cottages at one end of the High Street. The event itself was to happen in a separate field, and as I would have to unload boxes of books from the car, I was unsure about where to park. I suggested to Arthur that we park temporarily beside one of the thatched cottages so that I could get out and ask someone for advice. We did this. Arthur and I got out of the car and approached one of the stewards who had been directing the traffic in front of us. I spoke to him: 'Excuse me, I was just wondering –'

'Can't park there!'

The tone was peremptory and inflexible, chilled by distracted officialdom, the expression on the square, heavily browed face aggressive and slightly scornful. I tried once more.

'Yes, I realise that, but –'

'Carn chew read? There's a big sign right in front of your face telling you not to park there. Now, move your car before someone else moves it for you!'

This man's manner had now become really offensive. I heard a sardonic grunt from Arthur who was standing beside me. No more nor less than I would have expected, that grunt was clearly saying. I was distraught. What a terrible way to begin the day. Things couldn't get much worse than this, could they? Couldn't they? Oh, yes they could.

'Everything all right, Derek?' enquired a cultured voice from somewhere behind me.

It was a voice I recognised. This was one of the organisers. In fact, it was the man who had written and telephoned me over a year ago, inviting me to come and speak here. His name was Paul. Paul was a gentle, caring man, vicar of the parish church in this place.

'Trouble with parking, vicar,' said the steward, briskly censorious, 'these two people were trying to park over there by the house where they're not supposed to.'

'But, Derek,' said the minister, who had by now caught sight of my face, 'this is our main speaker for the afternoon. He'll be wanting to park down where the tents are on the main field.' He turned to us. 'Derek is from our church,' he said, 'and he's kindly helping out with the stewarding. He'll show you which way to go, and I'll see you down there in just a moment. So glad you've made it. Bye!'

Paul smiled as he hurried away, and we turned back to Derek. His face was now wreathed in good humour. It was as though a completely different, civilised, pleasantly spoken Derek had been hiding somewhere behind the monstrous persona that we had encountered only moments ago.

'I'm really sorry,' he said, 'I had no idea you were the speaker. I thought you were just one of the punters coming for the day. Come on, follow me and I'll show you how to get on to the main field.'

No doubt Derek thought he had made things all right by switching to this very different manner now that he knew I was not a 'punter.' But the darker, heavier cloud that I could sense had settled over my friend was a clear indication that he had not. I knew exactly what Arthur was thinking.

Why was it all right to be harsh and rude to someone who was 'only one of the punters', and then suddenly become all sweetness and light just because he turned out to be the speaker?

The answer was, of course, that it was most emphatically not all right. The only celebrities you are likely to find in God's kingdom are people like my mum, who cut elderly people's toenails and did all sorts of other things that no one else wanted to do, and until that is something we have truly understood, we would be well advised, except on the occasions when God commands us otherwise, to extend the same courtesy and goodwill to every person we meet.

The meeting progressed quite satisfactorily, but I knew that Arthur was not really engaging with any part of the proceedings. His view of the church as a place where you are bound to find hypocrisy and double standards had been confirmed by the very first person we encountered. From that moment he had shut his stubborn mind against anything that might have affected this view. On the way home I tried to say that Derek might have been having an off day, as we all do sometimes, that he probably had fine qualities we knew nothing of, and that, in any case, the Christian church caters exclusively for sinners. I could tell that Arthur remained sceptical. Thank goodness he was still close to Bridget and I. Silently I asked Jesus to go on looking out for moments when he might be able to meet our friend. I was sure he would. I hoped it would be soon.

Wolf: creature that will, according to a prophecy in the eleventh chapter of Isaiah, eventually lie down with the lamb. Charming and inspiring sentiment. If, however, I was the lamb, I would want to be absolutely sure that the time of fulfilment really had arrived before taking the earnestly expressed word of a hungry wolf as my guarantee of personal safety.

Wolf in sheep's clothing: clearly a danger to the flock, but not too difficult to spot, surely? Nowhere near as obvious as, say, a giraffe in ferret's clothing, I grant you, but you would think that the combination of

A B C D E F G H I J K L M N O P Q R S T U V W X Y Z

pointed ears, beady eyes, a lolling tongue, huge sharp teeth, entirely the wrong kind of feet and a tendency to howl at the moon and cock a leg against the water trough might be a bit of a giveaway. The problem is that some wolves have become remarkably skilful sheep impressionists. Beware!

Woman at the well: New Testament character who discovered how dangerous and unpredictable it can be to have a drink with a strange man.

Works: good deeds, as mentioned by the author of the book of James when he suggests the kind of exchange that might be conducted behind the spiritual bike sheds: 'You show me your faith and I'll show you my works . . .'

Worship leaders: (1) a fine body of sensitive, musically gifted men and women who enhance and enrich acts of worship and celebration in the church (2) egocentric bullies who either sing their own songs so that no one can join in, make people feel bad about themselves because they're not as happy as they should be, or go over their allocated time because they are so keen on the sound of their own voices. Yet another version of a chorus already mentioned under the heading **Subculture** illustrates the point:

> Father God I wonder
> why they bother with a speaker
> when they have a worship leader
> who's as wonderful as me.
> Now they won't be needing
> all that Holy Spirit leading

they have asked for twenty minutes
but my kind of talent knows no limits

I will sing for ever
I will sing for ever
I will sing for ever, for evermore
I will sing my praises
I will sing my praises
I will sing my praises for evermore.

XYLOPHONE

X

X-factor: crucial element that gives any person, experience or situation its individually positive attributes. Commonly associated nowadays with those television programmes that search for one star-quality performer out of thousands of applicants, and then produce someone who sounds like everyone else.

What is the X-factor in Christianity?

The answer to that question is Jesus, of course, but I have only recently begun to guess at the breadth and the depth and the beautiful ordinariness of that very simple fact. By this I do not mean that I have finally managed to get my head around abstruse and advanced theological concepts, nor have I at last found a way to live out the triumphant, joyful Christian life. On the contrary, in some ways I am more at sea in a storm than ever when it comes to all manner of things that I used to feel reasonably confident about. No, it is just that I have recently had two very interesting and significant dreams. Both of them were set in my grandmother's house.

If you have read the entry entitled **Patterns** in this book, you will already have heard about my Nana, my mother's mother. I am very nearly fifty-eight years old as I write, and I only knew my Nana for six of those years. That short, opening chapter of my life was well written and important.

Visiting her as a child involved a long and exciting double-decker bus journey from Tunbridge Wells to Heathfield, the town in East Sussex where she lived. I loved the journey there, sitting next to my mother on the top deck of the bus, pretending that the handrail was a steering wheel. I loved getting off at the top of Mutton Hall Hill, crossing the road and walking the hundred yards or so down to the house. Hurrying up the front path of 'Cabinda' to be greeted by Nana as though I was the most important person in the world remains one of the most thrillingly joy-filled memories of my life. On these occasions everything about the house and the town and the sky and the earth and the very air itself seemed to glitter and sparkle and sing with a joy that would have passed all understanding if I had ever stopped to consider such a foolishly irrelevant concept.

I loved being in the house, kneeling on a chair at the kitchen table making houses and lorries and boats with the big box of bits and pieces that Nana was always collecting for my brothers and I to play with. I loved messing about in the terraced garden where, as a child herself, my mother once told me, Nana had let her eat a picnic of jam sandwiches under a big umbrella in the rain, and I loved going to bed with one of the old stone hot-water bottles that Nana had never replaced with those floppy modern rubber ones. I loved being kissed goodnight by Nana and my mother. How could a night be made safer than that? I loved it all. It was pure joy.

Pure things are rare. Even the best and brightest of memories tend to have their dark spots. Perhaps because my grandmother died when I was so young, there are no detectable shadows to obscure my images of her and the house where she lived. It was all so, so wonderful. For various reasons home was something of a wilderness. Being with Nana in her house was Eden.

My two dreams took me back to Eden. In both cases I found myself in a place that I knew to be Nana's house, even though the physical details bore no resemblance to anything that I recall from my visits. Dreams are often like that, though. You simply know where you are.

I cannot tell you how deeply, tearfully satisfying it was to return to a place where there were no shadows, no nagging concerns about the inevitability of something going wrong, no heart-sinking certainty that, even if the long queue of resident worries should disappear, death would be waiting at the end of the line with a grin on its face to remind me that one day my body would die, and that if I turned out to be deluded in my faith, everything I was and everything I loved would be lost.

My dreams disarmed me with their strong, gentle insistence that I might wake even from the last and most dreadful nightmare of all, to a morning of fresh brightness that is carefully designed to last for ever.

Whenever people ask me what I want most in the entire world, I always give them the same answer. I want peace. I want to be at peace. I want the weight of my body, mind and spirit to be taken away from my consciousness, and for that space, that vacuum, to be filled with enveloping peace and rightness. I want to go home. I want to go home with those I care for and with my beloved enemies to a place where even those magical days in my grandmother's house are revealed to be little more than a suggestion or an introduction to the perfection that Jesus has won for us.

I thank God for my dreams. They have allowed me a little taste of the serenity that I yearn for. And what a good idea to let me have two rather than one. Like bookends in my spirit these intimations of joy are supporting the tattered record of my life and faith. They give me hope.

A B C D E F G H I J K L M N O P Q R S T U V W X Y Z

What is the X-factor in Christianity? The answer is Jesus, of course. But we must not forget to let people know that heaven will be – well, it will be heaven, and that, as far as we can tell, God wants nothing more than for us to be there to enjoy it with him. That is why he sent Jesus. That is the motivation behind the whole mysterious salvation plan. That is the heart of the Good News. That is the X-factor.

Life is tough for some of us, but we must go on dreaming our dreams, you and I. One of mine is that I shall see my Nana again. It will be marvellous, and we shall so enjoy being together again, but the reunion will not happen at her house.

Xylophone: (1) instrument occasionally played during church services (2) total irrelevance that gets dragged into every alphabetical list by cheating compilers because there are so few words beginning with 'X'.

Y

You: why not?

You never can tell: absolutely central fact and feature of Christian living. The moment you arrive at a fixed view about almost anything, there is a strong possibility that the Holy Spirit will turn your ideas upside down and leave you wondering how you could ever have arrived at your original view in the first place. Here is an example of this frequently repeated phenomenon:

I was in a cinema in Eastbourne, our nearest large town. The last time I had been in this place was for a special repeat showing of one of the

Star Wars films. On that evening there had been a memorable occurrence for those of us in the audience. Sir Alec Guinness uttered the following words in that unmistakable, resonantly hollow voice: 'The force will always be with you.' At that exact moment, precisely on cue, the entire electrical system in the cinema had ceased to function. The screen had faded to darkness and the soundtrack of the film had dwindled anti-climactically down into nothingness with a dull, disappointed whining sound.

I was actually wishing that the same thing would happen again. I would have liked something to go wrong in the cinema that evening. They were showing a film about the ministry of Jesus and I was hating it. The thing that made it all very strange was that I had been told many, many other Christians had really loved it. They thought it would be good for non-Christians to see it. Finding myself in a minority seemed to be almost a hobby of mine.

But really, who had been responsible for the casting in this film? See, there was their so-called Jesus up on the big screen before me. He looked like a skinny art student from a good home going through a brief and not very committed hippyish phase. If the makers of the film had been serious about expecting us to believe that this man had worked as a carpenter for two decades or more, then all I could say was that carpentry must have been a much softer option two thousand years ago than it was now. And his voice! How could you expect a man to speak with cosmic authority when he sounded as if he had been raised in a semi-detached villa in a forest of hanging baskets in Surbiton by very nice, mild people who advocated polite restraint in all encounters with other human beings?

As for the rest of the cast, well, take a look at them. These actors were blatantly just a bunch of people with clean feet, dressed in pyjamas and tea-towels, pretending to be disciples and crowd members and Pharisees and any other odd bods that needed to be seen hanging around in first century Palestine. I'd seen school productions that were more convincing. How could you possible take them seriously? Perhaps others could. I knew I couldn't. What on earth would non-Christians think of this pale, gutless version of the truth about the Son of God?

I began to rather enjoy hating the film. A satisfyingly high number of things were wrong with it. I started a little collection in my mind of criticisms to pass on to those friends who were most likely to agree with me.

I assumed that the general nature of my response would remain unaltered until the end of the film. I was wrong. Something else happened. Tears came to my eyes. Like meeting an old and dear friend in an unlikely place, I heard the sweet, familiar words of Jesus coming from the mouth of the young man from Surbiton and they melted my heart as they had always done. Once again I was overwhelmed by the incredible truth that God walked this gritty world as a man, that he spoke those words, and that he died an appalling death because I could not go home unless he did. The words rang like bells on Christmas morning to announce that God is expressing good will towards men, and that Jesus is the evidence.

I still hated the film. Some of it was very silly. Some of it was absurd. I never wanted to see it again. But I found myself hoping that when others heard those famous words, especially those who were not followers of Jesus, they would sense the life and power that had made me cry, despite myself, that evening in a cinema in Eastbourne.

Youth Groups: collections of young people who, in a church context, can bring a great deal of joy, puzzlement and occasional annoyance to their parents and to those who run such groups. The joy, for many Christian parents in particular, is simply in the fact that their offspring have found a well supervised, sausage-sizzling, chorus singing, Scripture discussing, housepartying way of filling in all that dangerous free time. Wise parents will be aware that involvement in such activities is by no means a guarantee of genuine spiritual engagement or progress. On the other side of the same coin there are children and teenagers who, although unable to fit comfortably into conventional church groups, may well meet Jesus on a completely different path.

The puzzlement is what usually precedes the annoyance. I have met and talked with many leaders of church youth groups who are confused by the way in which the young people they work with behave in bizarrely different ways on different occasions. At a Sunday meeting after church, for instance, they might be deeply, sincerely engrossed in prayer and worship, and then, five or six days later on a youth group excursion they are out in boats half drowning each other as well as damaging and destroying equipment belonging to the owner of the boats.

'How can it be possible,' asked the frazzled youth leader who had experienced this particular problem, 'for people to be so devout and committed one day, and then turn into irresponsible hooligans within a week? Maybe I shouldn't let it affect me, but I get so cross!'

The answer, of course, is that teenagers retain all the central and predictable characteristics of their wonderful, dreadful race, whether or not they are Christians. My own children always wanted to be good, loving children who made their parents proud of them. At the same time they wanted to be bad, thoughtless children who experimented with things that would make their parents less than proud of them. That is how it works, and dealing with this inevitable contrast as a parent or a youth leader requires the patience, judgement and juggling skills of a saintly genius with a circus background. Frightening, isn't it? I made mistakes all the time.

Interestingly, those very strict Christian communities known as The Amish, mainly based in America, cope with this phenomenon better than most of us. Amish young people are allowed a period in their teenage years known as the 'Running around' time, during which a more or less blind eye is turned to their behavioural excesses. At the end of this time

A B C D E F G H I J K L M N O P Q R S T U V W X Y Z

they are expected to get baptised, settle down and make a serious long term commitment to the Christian community. And it appears to work.

The bottom line, as ever, seems to be love. 'Love them and keep your mouth shut' was the best parenting advice I ever got. I didn't follow it, of course, but it did sometimes make me keep quiet when I was about to say some of those terrible wounding words that can never be taken back. Youth leaders and parents will know exactly what I mean.

Ywam: Why indeed?

A B C D E F G H I J K L M N O P Q R S T U V W X Y Z

A B C D E F G H I J K L M N O P Q R S T U V W X Y Z

Z

Zacchaeus: when Jesus came to tea this tax collector gave away half his wealth, which must have left him a bit short. Must have been well worth seeing, as he already looked like Danny DeVito in a tea-towel.

Zap flap: not sure, but probably a small hinged door in the gates of heaven through which dirty stop-out believers or angels can find their way back in after midnight.

Zechariah: father of John the Baptist who was so gob-smacked by hearing that his prayers were about to be answered that his gob stopped working altogether.

Zephaniah: a book of the Old Testament that, as far as I know, has only ever been read by me. Concludes with a verse that was a turning point in my life at a time when things looked very dark indeed. Verse twenty concludes with these words:

'"Behold, I will restore your fortunes before your very eyes," saith the Lord.'

And that, I am pleased to say, is exactly what he did, not in terms of excessive amounts of money, but in all the ways that really count. I have nothing against money, mind you. In fact, I have often wondered how I would survive the temptation to become filthy rich in exchange for my soul. Recently I had a chance to find out. Whether this was a dream or whether it actually happened is not something I can be absolutely sure about, but it doesn't really matter.

It all began when the doorbell rang at precisely ten o'clock one autumn morning when I was sitting in my study. I thought it must be the milkman calling for his money. I was pleased in a way. I have a love-hate relationship with anything that interrupts what I risibly call my flow of work. Often, at that time of the morning, I will be hunched over my keyboard, growling discontentedly at two or three solid slabs of prose sitting cold and dead on the screen of my computer. These dull rectangles will have to be enlivened or dumped later in the day, but they are a crucial part of my daily search for a doorway into that elusive, exhilarating world

A B C D E F G H I J K L M N O P Q R S T U V W X Y Z

where words take off and I am allowed to ride them as they fly. During the slab phase just about any interruption is more than welcome.

When the words do begin to take wings there is a sense in which interruptions hardly matter. My heart is rippling with the excitement of rediscovered fluency. Even the stolid figure of our milkman can be transfigured to the degree that he acquires an aura of vivid significance. He would be amazed if he knew.

On this particular morning I had been working since nine o'clock on a short story commissioned by a Christian magazine. The brief was a broad one. I was free to write about anything as long as it had a Christian slant and dealt with the theme of Contrast. I had not got very far. Half a slab was all I had to show for an hour's growling and too much black coffee. That knock on the door was a welcome sound. Even an untransfigured milkman would be a blessed relief. Standing up, I fumbled some money out of my back pocket and headed for the front door.

It was not the milkman at all. It was a very smart young man in his mid-twenties carrying a leather briefcase. He was around six feet tall, strikingly well groomed and wearing a beautifully tailored charcoal suit. A charming smile illuminated his dark, evenly featured face as I pulled open the door. It was followed by a quizzically raised eyebrow as his gaze registered the two crumpled currency notes in my outstretched hand.

'Oh, sorry.' I smiled as I tucked the money back into my pocket. 'I thought it was going to be the milkman. You're definitely not the milkman, are you?'

'Mister Plass, isn't it?'

The voice was polite and pleasantly modulated. Bound to be selling something, I thought.

'Adrian Plass, yes, what can I do for you? If it's to do with changing our electricity or gas supplier I'm not interested, and I'm in the middle of – '

'No, it's about your ministry, Mister Plass. My name is Paris Morpeth. Forgive me for not making an appointment, but I have a proposition to put to you and time is very short. Can you spare fifteen minutes?'

Scratch a Christian writer and speaker, and you'll find a self-employed worker who is as keen to eat food and wear clothes and keep warm in the winter as the next person. I am happy to do all sorts of things for little material reward, or even for nothing, but if people throw money at me I will always give serious consideration to the proposition of catching it. This young man might have something lucrative to offer, and even if he hadn't – well, a quarter of an hour in his company must surely be marginally more interesting than battling with a story that refused to be written.

'Call me Adrian, please. Come in out of the cold. I'll make us a drink.'

A few minutes later we were seated in my little study, me in the comfortable upright red chair that I use for writing, and the impressively

A B C D E F G H I J K L M N O P Q R S T U V W X Y Z

named Paris Morpeth occupying the old flowery armchair in the corner, one of his elegantly trousered legs crossed over the other. We sipped from our mugs of coffee for a moment in silence.

'So,' I ventured at last, 'what can I do for you?'

Reaching down, the young man flicked a couple of catches on his expensive briefcase. From inside he drew out a small rectangular piece of paper, and leaning forward, offered it to me.

'Would you be kind enough to glance at this?'

I took the slip of paper and studied it carefully. It was a cheque from a major high street bank, made out to me for the sum of five million pounds.

'To answer your question, Adrian,' said Morpeth, leaning back easily in his chair, 'we would like you to accept this cheque as payment for certain services, the nature of which I shall explain in a few moments. In the meantime, let me assure you that the cheque and the offer we are making are one hundred per cent genuine. I should point out, however, that this proposition is valid only for the period during which I am with you here today. At the moment when I leave your house the offer, if you have seen fit to refuse it, will be automatically withdrawn and never under any circumstances repeated.'

Morpeth paused. His dark eyes were fixed on mine, but with no easily identifiable expression.

'So,' he continued, 'shall I take back the cheque and leave immediately, or shall I tell you what we want in return for five million pounds?'

Before I started this writing and speaking business I worked with difficult, sometimes violent teenagers in a variety of institutions, including secure units. I encountered sights, sounds and conversations that would appear shocking or strange to most people. In these environments they were more or less commonplace. It was a fact that some kind of logical reason, albeit a twisted one at times, would always emerge in the end, even for the most startlingly surreal and illogical set of circumstances. I had learned to lean back instead of forward, as it were, on these occasions, and that was what I decided to do now. These inexplicable things, the immaculate Paris Morpeth and his ridiculous cheque, must mean something. If I stayed calm and sat tight, there was a good chance that, sooner or later, I would find out what that meaning was. I dropped the slip of paper with all its noughts carelessly onto the desk beside me before replying.

'Something to do with my ministry, you said?'

'Yes, that's correct. Writing, speaking, broadcasting. In fact, any or all forms of public communication on the subject of your Christian faith.'

I spread my hands and shook my head in puzzled enquiry.

'Yes, but what about it? What exactly do you want me to do?'

'Nothing. Do nothing. We want you to stop. We would like to pay you to not do it any more. Not ever, from this moment until the day of your death. We wish your ministry to end.'

Humour him.

'And if I agree to do that, you will pay me five million pounds?'

Morpeth nodded.

'The money would be yours to dispose of as you wish. I am aware, for instance, that you have been involved with a Christian aid agency in recent years. You visited a small, poverty stricken village in Zambia only eighteen months ago. You said that it broke your heart to witness such suffering and hunger. With one fifth of the money we are offering you, the lives of those people could be radically changed for the better.' He raised his chin challengingly. 'So do it. We can make it possible. Remember that verse from the book of James that you so frequently quote to your audiences? True religion is about looking after widows and orphans. Something like that, is it not? Okay. Live it. Make it come true. Show you mean it. Look after them. Take the money.'

Humour him for just a little longer.

'Mister Morpeth – '

'Paris, please.'

'Paris.' Reaching over I picked up the cheque once more and waved it like a little flag. 'This is really nothing but a piece of paper. You can write anything at all on a piece of paper. I could write you a cheque for any amount you like. Pay Paris Morpeth fifty million pounds. Easy. But it wouldn't mean anything. In any case – '

Pushing the palm of his left hand towards me like a traffic cop, Morpeth delved into his open briefcase again, pulled out a large brown-paper package and handed it across. On examination it turned out to be one very large envelope folded over on itself.

'Please open it,' said Morpeth.

I slit the sealed end open with a paper knife from the pot on my desk and peered inside. The envelope was stuffed with fifty-pound notes. Hundreds of them. I had never seen so much money at one time in my life. Withdrawing one of the wads of currency, I studied it with silent intensity, as though it was a fresh wound in my hand.

'There's a few hundred thousand in there.' The young man's tone was conversational. 'Take that for now. It's yours. Extra money. A bonus in advance. Use it in any way you wish. A sign of our goodwill. An indication that we really do mean business.'

I realised that my jaw was hanging open. I closed it. A shiver of sudden fear passed through me, only to be lost in a wave of equally sudden but unexpected greed. Wodges, chunks, crunchy stacks of fifty-pound notes. Not to mention a cheque for five million pounds that might, for some crazy, lunatic reason, deliver exactly what this man was promising.

'Let me save you some time,' said Morpeth, a disarming smile on his handsome features, 'by telling you that this is not a test. Not a joke. Not a swindle or a scam. Oh, and in case you wondered, I am not the devil in modern dress, and this is not some contemporary bid to purchase your soul, even if such a thing were possible. No, Adrian, this is simply – business. I represent a body of folk who believe their best interests would be served by the discontinuation of your activities in what we might term the public Christian world. I would ask you not to waste your time or mine by asking for further information about my employers or their reasons for making this offer. I am permitted to say nothing more on that subject.' He raised a finger as if recalling an important point that had been missed. 'By the way, you would of course be perfectly free to continue involvement with your own church in any capacity and to whatever extent that you wished.'

I was out of my depth, struggling to find a way back to the surface, to the fresh air of reason and sanity.

'Look, let's suppose for one moment,' I said slowly, 'that this is all genuine. Mad, of course, but genuine. You and your – employers. You seriously do want to give me a small fortune in exchange for stopping all the Christian stuff I do. Surely it must have occurred to you, or them, that I might feel very encouraged by all this? I mean, presumably I'm doing something amazingly right if you're willing to pay me millions of pounds to stop?'

Morpeth nodded serenely. My impression was that he had just crossed my comment off a mental checklist.

'That is for you to decide, Adrian,' he replied. 'Perhaps the exercise of your ministry will do more than five and a half million pounds' worth of good in the limited period of your working life that remains. Who knows? What we do both know is that you are fifty-seven years old, that you have minimal financial resources, and that there are times when you experience total doubt about the things that you speak and write about with such passion. Am I wrong? You value truth. You wear that claim as others wear a badge. Speak the truth about this.'

I stared at him, licking dry lips before speaking. My voice, when it finally emerged, must have sounded very small.

'No, you're not wrong. I do sometimes wonder if the whole thing's a gigantic mistake. But I've said that as publicly as I've said everything else. It's part of being an individual human being who happens to also be a – '

'Is it not also true,' interrupted Morpeth, leaning forward and speaking with increased animation, 'that there are dark and dreadful moments when you suspect that you have given more than twenty years to pursuing a narrow way that finally leads to nothing, nowhere, no reward at all. All that trying to be good. All that fighting against temptation. All that investment in the notion that sacrifice will be ultimately worthwhile because an absolute expression of love and goodness waits to welcome you beyond the grave. What a waste if you are deluded. And what a farce! The severely short-sighted but very vocal leading a host of equally short-sighted towards some hypothetical healer of blindness who does not exist.'

He sank back again, flicked a speck of invisible dust from his sleeve, and continued in the calm tones he had used previously.

'We are offering you more than five million pounds. Every one of those pounds is as concrete and genuine as the flesh and blood hand you are using to grip our money at this moment.'

I took a deep breath and released it slowly. There was indeed a seductive weightiness about the fibrous block of money wedged between the thumb and fingers of my right hand. Morpeth watched me without blinking for a moment before continuing.

'Adrian, you might possibly have fifteen or twenty years of active life remaining to you. Perhaps less. Possibly a great deal less. Take the money. You will never have cause to agonise over the reality of your wealth. Do good with it. Buy things. Help your family as you've always dreamed of doing. Be comfortable. If the God you have enthused about for twenty years does exist, and if his nature is as loving and forgiving as you have so strongly maintained, how can you lose? Pay the cash and the cheque into your bank account today. In five days you will still be a Christian, but you will also be a multi-millionaire.'

Shooting the cuff of his jacket sleeve, he frowned at the face of a gleamingly expensive watch.

'Two minutes,' he said. 'You have two minutes in which to make a decision, and then I must leave. No more discussion. No more questions. Make up your mind. Continue with your ministry, or grasp your only opportunity to become fabulously wealthy. I have nothing more to say.'

When I closed the door on Paris Morpeth's immaculately clothed back a few minutes later I was as rich and no richer than I had been before he arrived. Returning to my study I asked myself why I had turned down the possibility of receiving such a vast amount of money. Some would think me quite mad. The answer was not simple.

Morpeth had been right about me sometimes disappearing down a black hole of doubt, but that was only a small part of the story. I have known a lot of genuine, leaping happiness over the years of my journey with Jesus, and that has been as genuine as the despair and the darkness. Grotty times and great times and everything you can conceive of in between.

What that puzzled observer would need to understand is that this thing, this relationship with Jesus – if he exists, and if all the other stuff I go on about really is true – it makes me laugh. It makes me cry as well. So many times I have wept and wept because I feel things right down there inside the part of me that is always trying to be authentic and stay clean. I weep because of what they did to him. Because of what they still do to him. Because of what I do to him. Because I want him to be closer. Because I am angry with him. Because I cannot understand him. Because

I feel his pain and his yearning and his unstoppable love for hearts and bodies and minds and lives that are broken and lost. My mind may lose its way from time to time, but my heart is a bruised believer.

And he gave me a job to do, this Jesus who may or may not exist. Everyone who is willing to have a go is trusted with a special part of the big picture, and perhaps that big, mysterious, beautiful picture will never have a chance to be properly finished if my silly little bit turns out to be missing in the end. During that two minutes allowed for my decision I realised that, ultimately, all I want is to meet the Son of God in heaven at last – assuming there is such a place, of course – and see him smile, and hear him say, 'You messed things up here and there, Adrian, but you did have a go at the job I gave you to do, and I appreciate it. Thank you. Come on in.'

Paris Morpeth was right about one other thing. I expect I would have been forgiven in the end if I had taken the cash, but that is not the point. How could I have borne to meet Jesus, who saw his own appalling job so bravely through to the bitter, miserable glorious end, and not be able to look him in the face?

I went on to embody the events of that morning, real or unreal, in the story I was trying to write, and if my readers were looking for a contrast, then there certainly was one there for them to consider. Before Morpeth's visit I could never have put any kind of specific price on my faith. Now I knew – I know – that it is worth five and a half million pounds, at least.

Ziklag: (1) city burned by King David in the first book of Samuel (2) extreme tiredness and other bodily effects felt in the few hours following arrival after a long-haul journey across time zones in a Jumbo-zik.